15 TOP HITS
FOR EASY PIANO

ISBN 978-1-4768-1414-8

HAL•LEONARD®
CORPORATION

7777 W. BLUEMOUND RD. P.O. BOX 13819 MILWAUKEE, WI 53213

For all works contained herein:
Unauthorized copying, arranging, adapting, recording, Internet posting, public performance,
or other distribution of the printed music in this publication is an infringement of copyright.
Infringers are liable under the law.

Visit Hal Leonard Online at
www.halleonard.com

S0-AKO-130

3
BRIGHTER THAN THE SUN
COLBIE CAILLAT

17
FIREWORK
KATY PERRY

12
GLAD YOU CAME
THE WANTED

24
JUST A KISS
LADY ANTEBELLUM

32
JUST THE WAY YOU ARE
BRUNO MARS

38
MOVES LIKE JAGGER
MAROON 5
featuring CHRISTINA AGUILERA

56
OURS
TAYLOR SWIFT

47
PARADISE
COLDPLAY

64
POKER FACE
LADY GAGA

76
ROLLING IN THE DEEP
ADELE

84
SOMEONE LIKE YOU
ADELE

69
STRONGER (WHAT DOESN'T KILL YOU)
KELLY CLARKSON

92
A THOUSAND YEARS
CHRISTINA PERRI

100
WE ARE YOUNG
FUN.

106
WHAT MAKES YOU BEAUTIFUL
ONE DIRECTION

BRIGHTER THAN THE SUN

Words and Music by COLBIE CAILLAT
and RYAN TEDDER

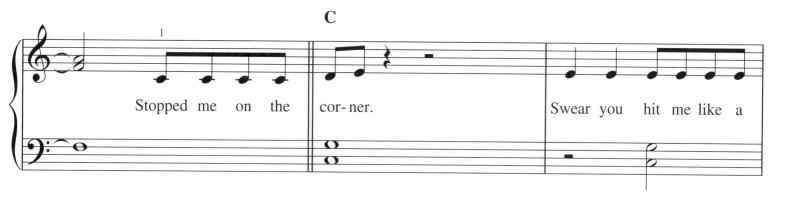

Stopped me on the cor-ner. Swear you hit me like a

vi - sion I, I, I was-n't ex - pect - ing,

but who am I to tell fate where it's s'pposed __ to go

Copyright © 2011 Plummy Lou Music (BMI) and Write 2 Live Publishing (ASCAP)
All Rights on behalf of Write 2 Live Publishing Administered by Kobalt Music Publishing America, Inc.
International Copyright Secured   All Rights Reserved

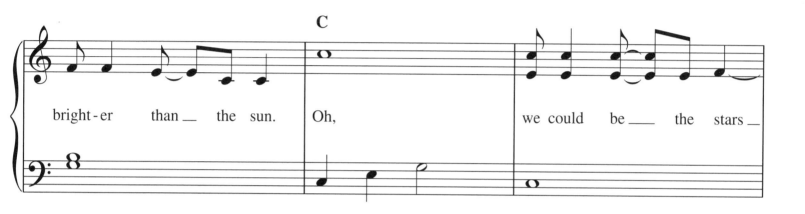

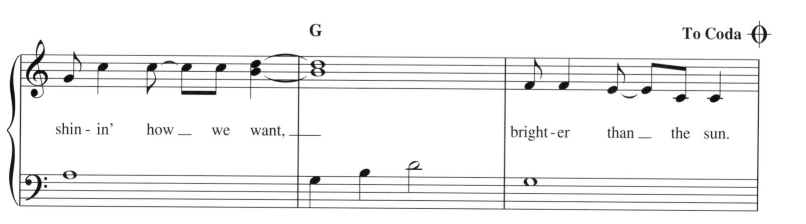

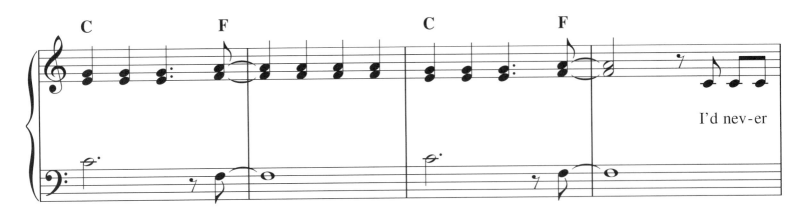

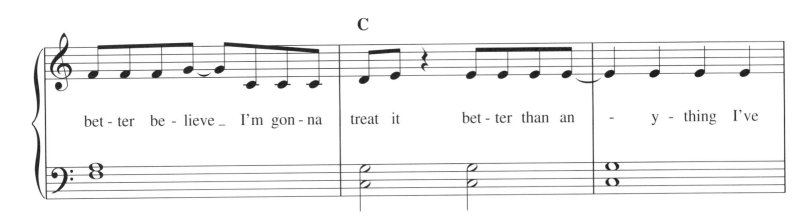

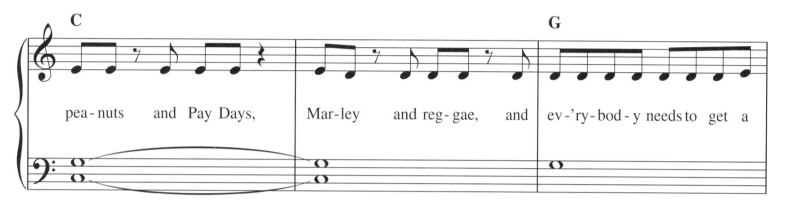

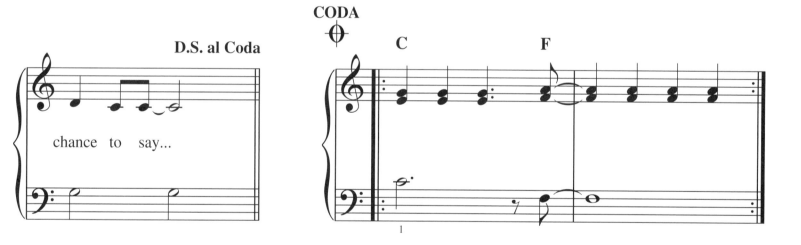

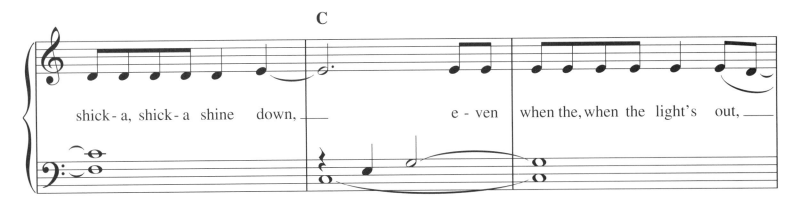

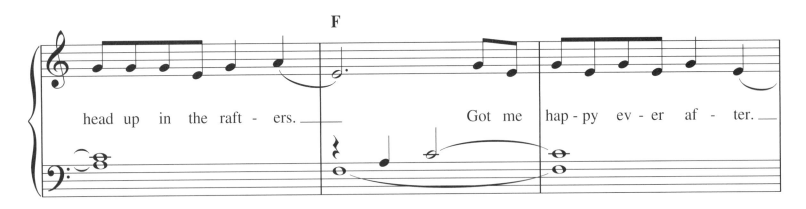

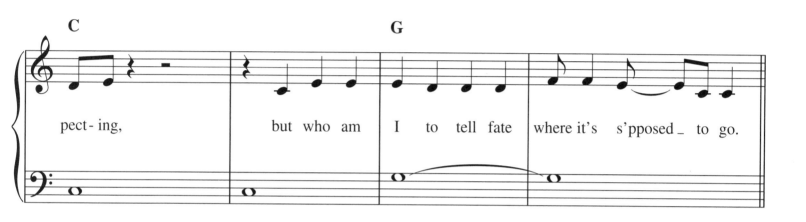

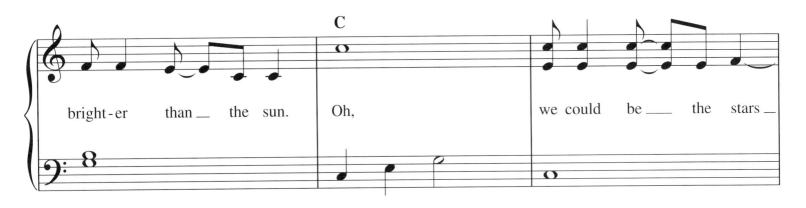

bright-er   than __ the sun.   Oh,   we could   be ___   the   stars __

__   fall - in'   from __   the   sky, _____

shin - in'   how __   we   want, _____   bright-er   than __   the   sun.

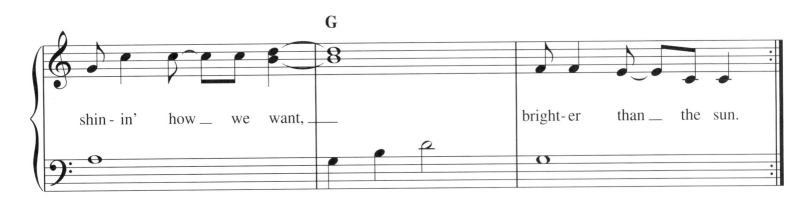

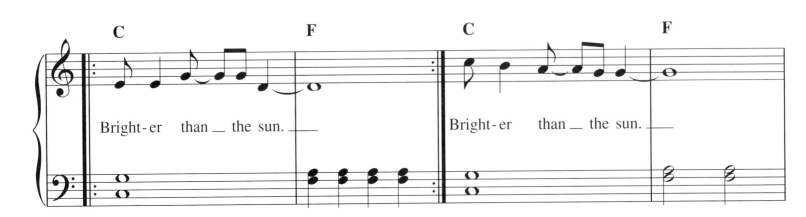

Bright-er   than __   the sun. ___   Bright-er   than __   the sun. ___

Oh, this is how __ it starts. ___ Light-ning strikes __ the heart; ___

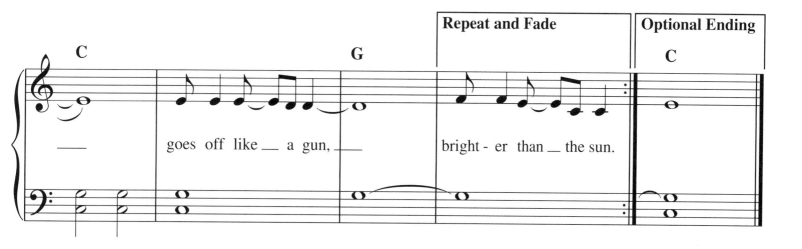

Repeat and Fade | **Optional Ending**

__ goes off like __ a gun, ___ bright-er than __ the sun.

GLAD YOU CAME

Words and Music by STEVE MAC,
WAYNE HECTOR and EDWARD DREWETT

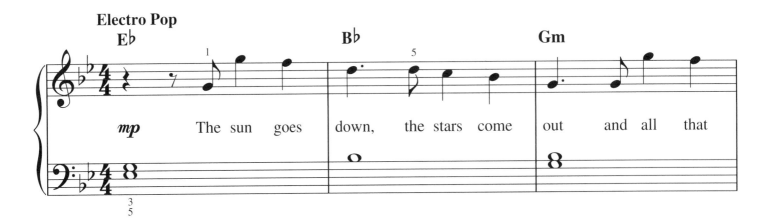

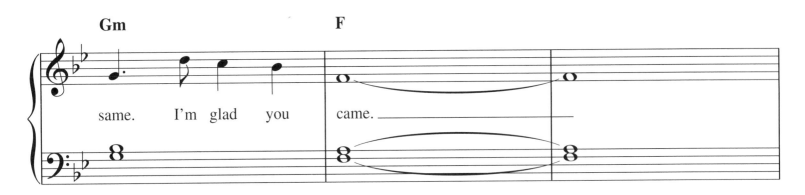

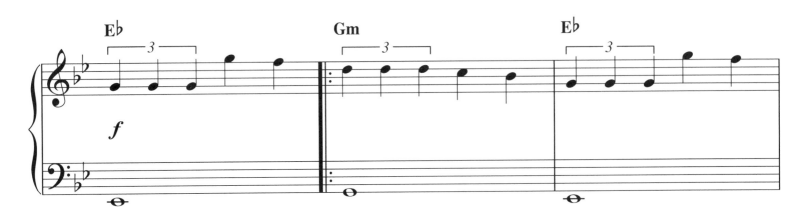

Copyright © 2011 by Rokstone Music, Warner/Chappell Music Publishing Ltd., WB Music Corp. and Warner-Tamerlane Publishing Corp.
All Rights for Rokstone Music in the U.S. Administered by Songs Of Peer, Ltd.
All Rights for Rokstone Music in the world excluding the U.S. Administered by Peermusic (UK) Limited
All Rights Reserved   Used by Permission

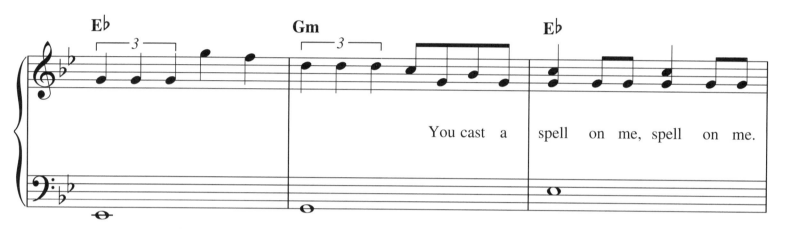

You cast a spell on me, spell on me.

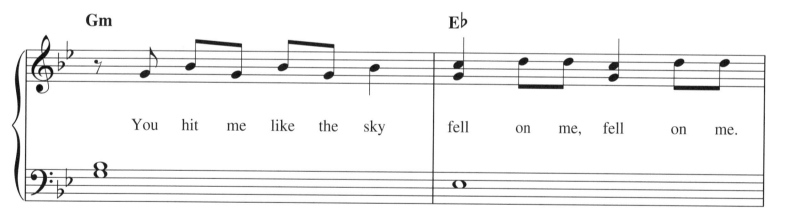

You hit me like the sky fell on me, fell on me.

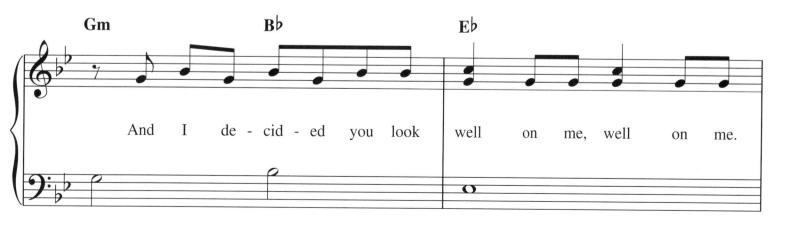

And I de-cid-ed you look well on me, well on me.

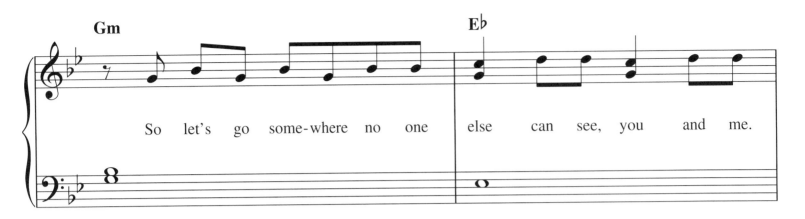

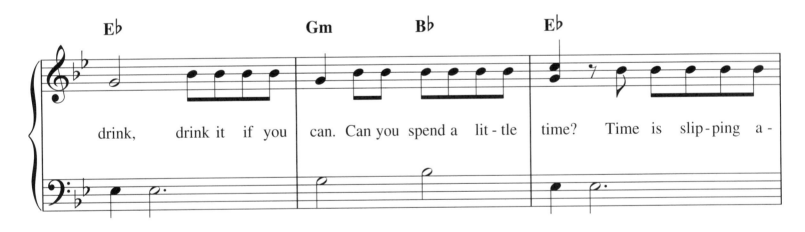

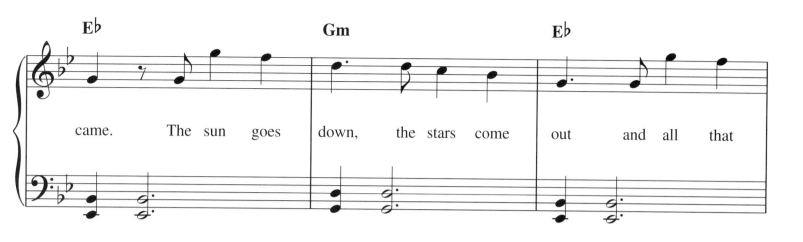

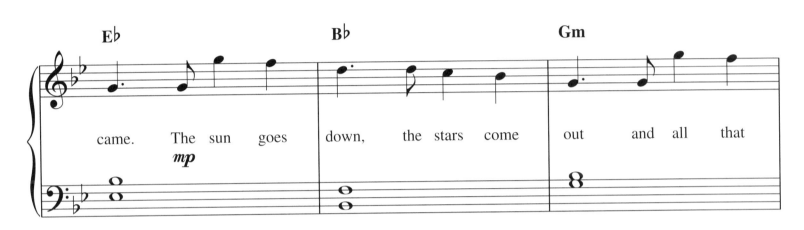

FIREWORK

Words and Music by MIKKEL ERIKSEN,
TOR ERIK HERMANSEN,
ESTHER DEAN, KATY PERRY
and SANDY WILHELM

Dance Pop

Do you ev-er feel   like a plas-tic bag,
You don't have to feel   like a wast-ed space.

drift-ing through the wind,   want-ing to start a-gain? __
You're o-rig-i-nal,   can-not be re-placed. __

Do you ev-er feel,   feel so pa-per thin,   like a house of cards,
If you on-ly knew   what the fu-ture holds,   af-ter a hur-ri-cane

© 2010 EMI MUSIC PUBLISHING LTD., PEERMUSIC III, LTD., DAT DAMN DEAN MUSIC, 2412 LLC,
WB MUSIC CORP., WHEN I'M RICH YOU'LL BE MY BITCH and DIPIU MUSIC PUBLISHING S.R.L.
All Rights for EMI MUSIC PUBLISHING LTD. in the U.S. and Canada Controlled and Administered by EMI APRIL MUSIC INC.
All Rights for DAT DAMN DEAN MUSIC and 2412 LLC Controlled and Administered by PEERMUSIC III, LTD.
All Rights for WHEN I'M RICH YOU'LL BE MY BITCH Controlled and Administered by WB MUSIC CORP.
All Rights Reserved   International Copyright Secured   Used by Permission

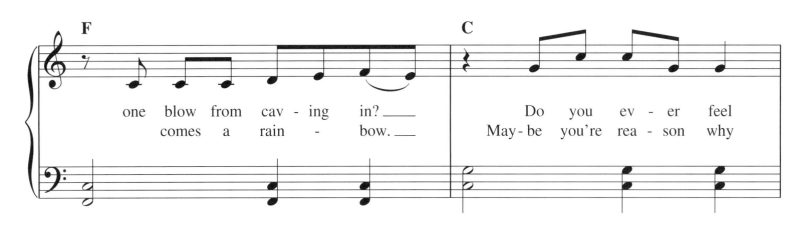

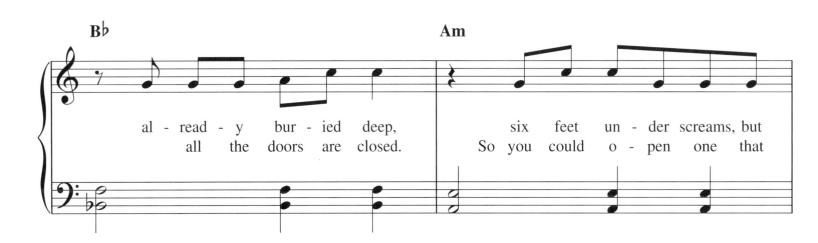

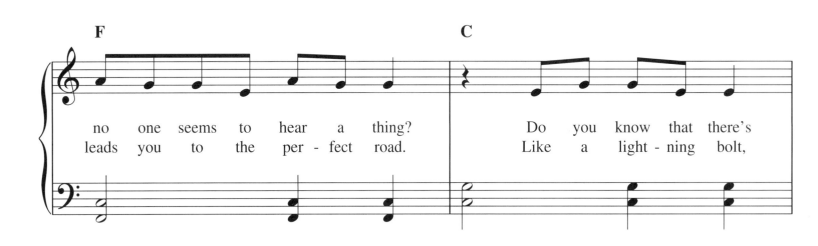

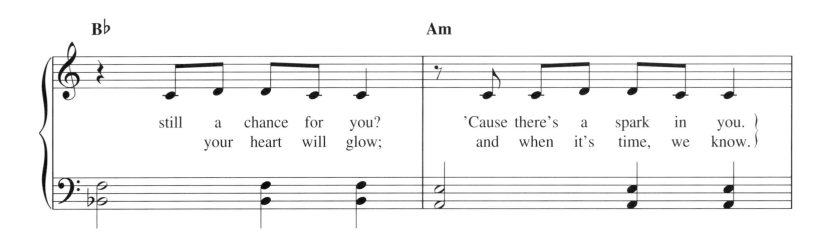

19

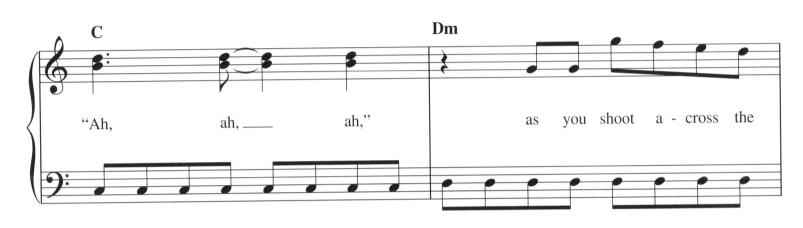

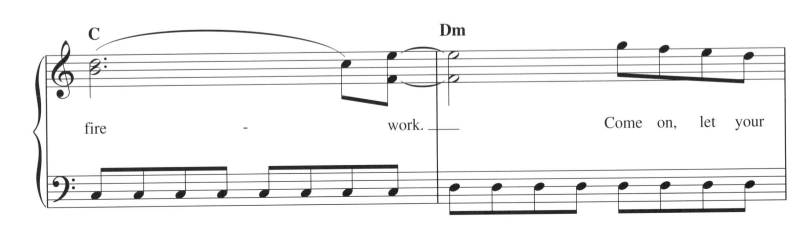

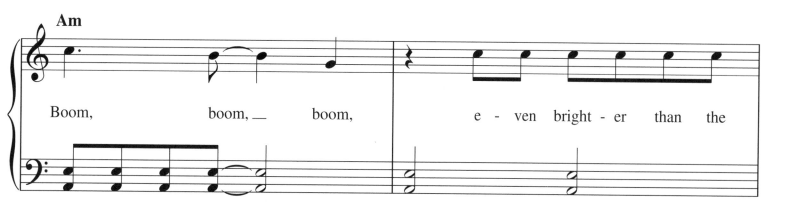

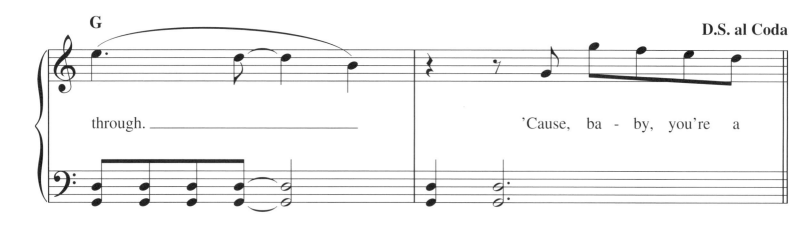

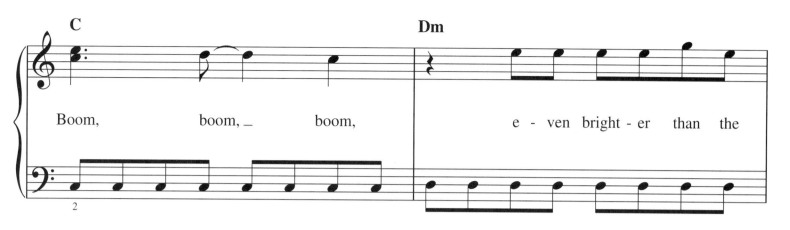

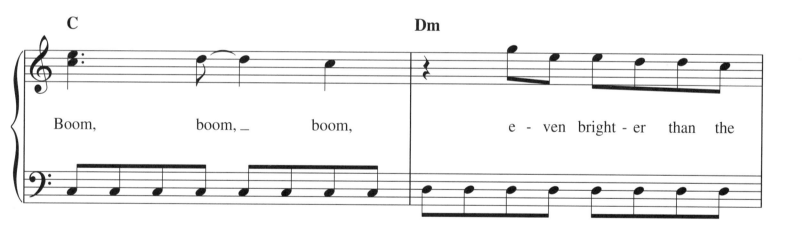

JUST A KISS

Words and Music by HILLARY SCOTT,
DALLAS DAVIDSON, CHARLES KELLEY
and DAVE HAYWOOD

© 2011 EMI FORAY MUSIC, HILLARY DAWN SONGS, EMI BLACKWOOD MUSIC INC., STRING STRETCHER MUSIC,
WARNER-TAMERLANE PUBLISHING CORP., RADIOBULLETSPUBLISHING and DWHAYWOOD MUSIC
All Rights for HILLARY DAWN SONGS Controlled and Administered by EMI FORAY MUSIC
All Rights for STRING STRETCHER MUSIC Controlled and Administered by EMI BLACKWOOD MUSIC INC.
All Rights for RADIOBULLETSPUBLISHING and DWHAYWOOD MUSIC Controlled and Administered by WARNER-TAMERLANE PUBLISHING CORP.
All Rights Reserved   International Copyright Secured   Used by Permission

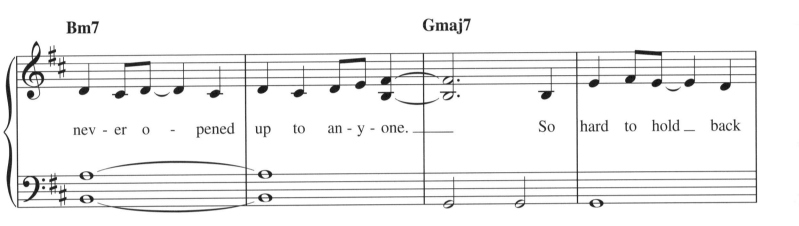

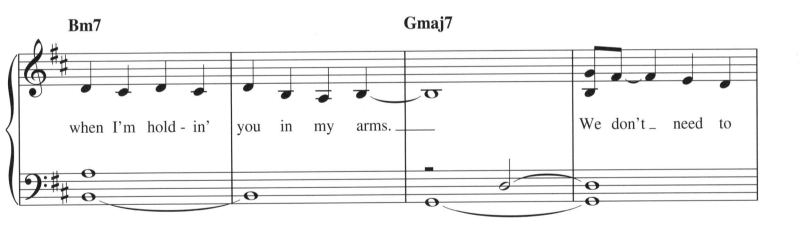

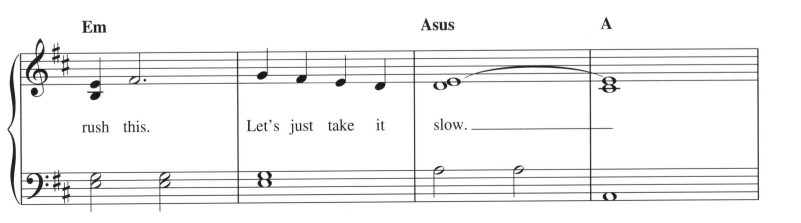

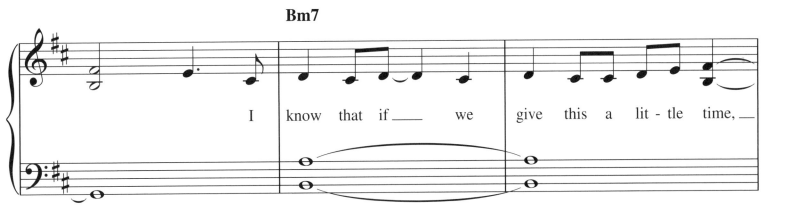

we wan-na find. ____ It's nev-er ___ felt so real. No, it's

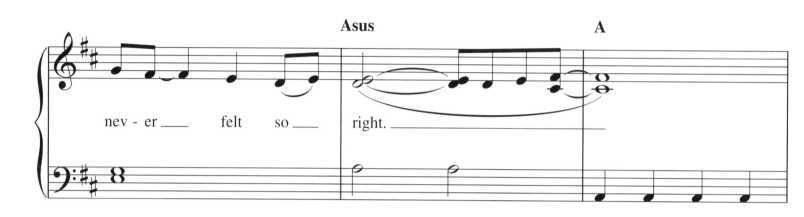

nev - er ___ felt so ___ right. ____

Just a kiss on your lips in the moon - light, ___ just a touch of the

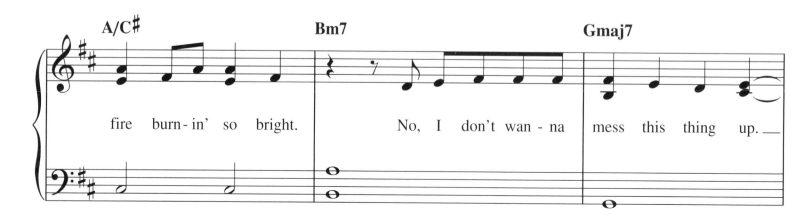

fire burn-in' so bright. No, I don't wan - na mess this thing up. __

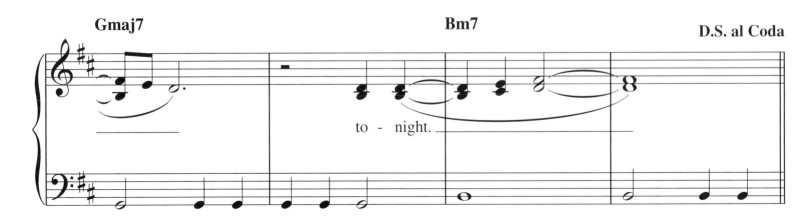

31

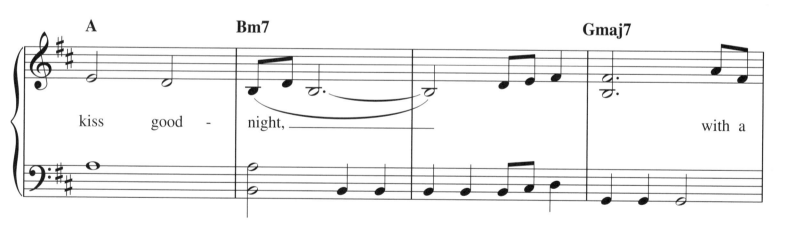

JUST THE WAY YOU ARE

Words and Music by BRUNO MARS,
ARI LEVINE, PHILIP LAWRENCE,
KHARI CAIN and KHALIL WALTON

Moderate Hip-Hop groove

© 2010 MARS FORCE MUSIC, BUGHOUSE, NORTHSIDE INDEPENDENT MUSIC PUBLISHING, LLC, TOY PLANE MUSIC, ART FOR ART'S SAKE MUSIC,
MUSIC FAMAMANEM LP, ROC NATION MUSIC, UNIVERSAL MUSIC CORP., DRY RAIN ENTERTAINMENT and KHALIL WALTON PUBLISHING DESIGNEE
All Rights for MARS FORCE MUSIC, BUGHOUSE, TOY PLANE MUSIC and ART FOR ART'S SAKE MUSIC Administered by BUG MUSIC, INC., a BMG CHRYSALIS COMPANY
All Rights for MUSIC FAMAMANEM LP and ROC NATION MUSIC Controlled and Administered by EMI APRIL MUSIC INC.
All Rights for DRY RAIN ENTERTAINMENT Controlled and Administered by UNIVERSAL MUSIC CORP.
All Rights Reserved   Used by Permission

Oh, her eyes, — her eyes — make the stars look like they're not shin - in'.

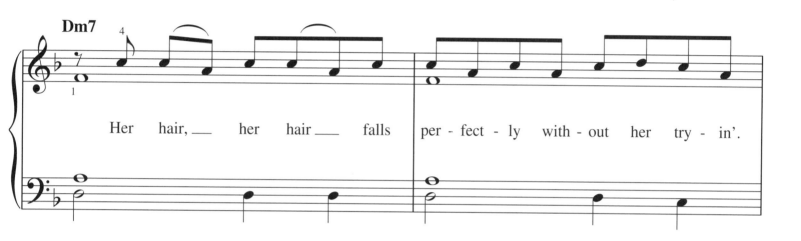

Dm7

Her hair, — her hair — falls per - fect - ly with - out her try - in'.

F/B♭   **F**

She's so beau - ti - ful, and I tell her ev - 'ry day.

Yeah. I know, — I know — when I

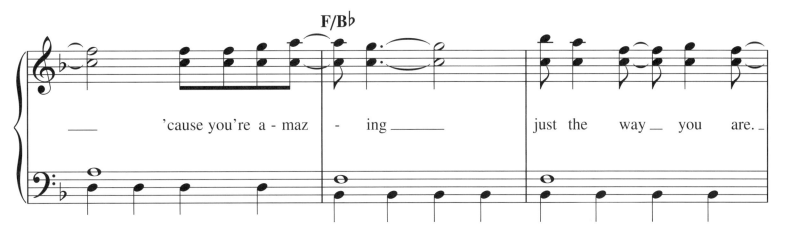

'cause you're a - maz - ing _____ just the way _ you are. _

_____ And when you smile, _

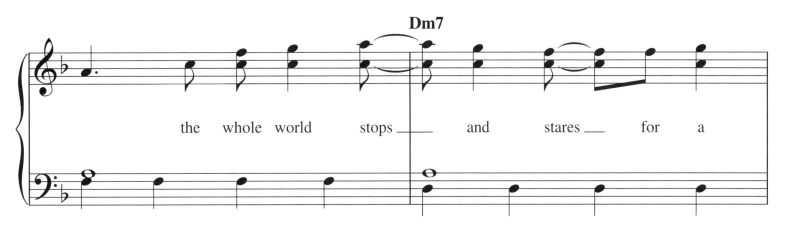

the whole world stops _ and stares _ for a

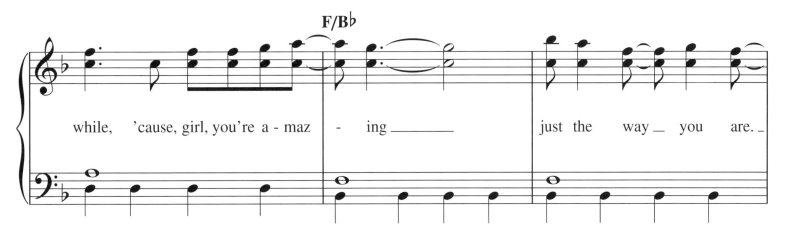

while, 'cause, girl, you're a - maz - ing _____ just the way _ you are. _

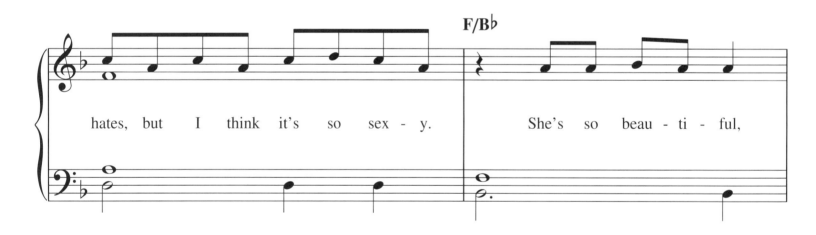

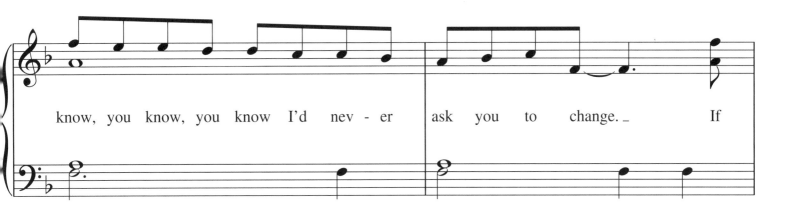

know, you know, you know I'd nev - er ask you to change. _ If

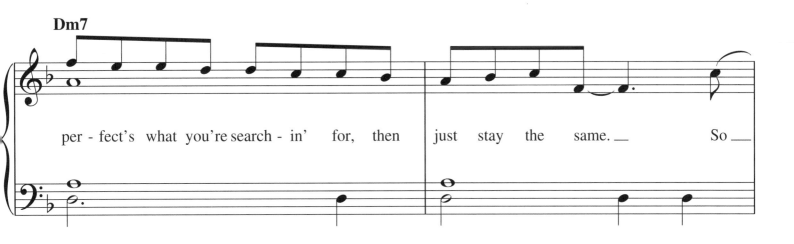

Dm7

per - fect's what you're search - in' for, then just stay the same. _ So _

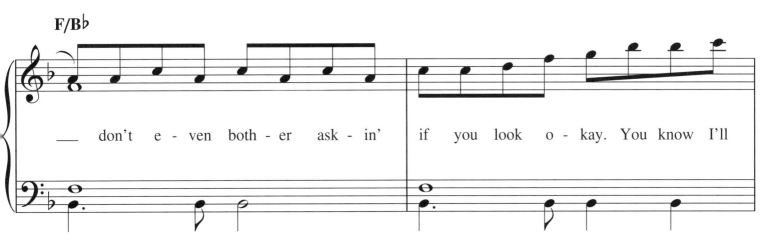

F/B♭

_ don't e - ven both - er ask - in' if you look o - kay. You know I'll

F

say: _____ When I see your face, _

D.S. al Coda

CODA

Yeah. _

MOVES LIKE JAGGER

Words and Music by ADAM LEVINE,
BENJAMIN LEVIN, AMMAR MALIK
and JOHAN SCHUSTER

With energy

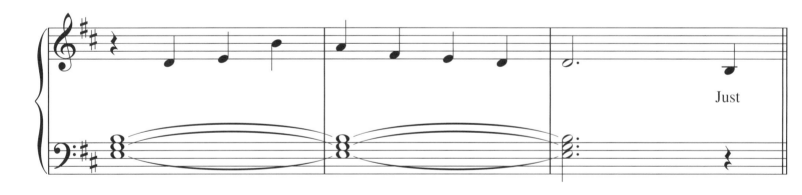

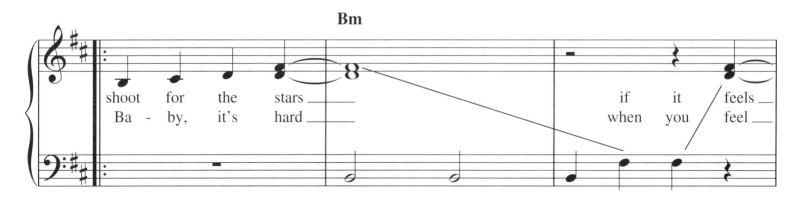

Copyright © 2011 by Universal Music - Careers, Sudgee Music, Where Da Kasz At, Matza Ball Music, Maru Cha Cha and Maratone AB
All Rights for Sudgee Music Administered by Universal Music - Careers
All Rights for Where Da Kasz At, Matza Ball Music, Maru Cha Cha and Maratone AB Administered by Kobalt Music Publishing America, Inc.
International Copyright Secured   All Rights Reserved

right, and aim for my heart
like you're bro - ken and scarred,

if you feel like it. Take me a - way
noth - in' feels like right. But when you're with me,

Em7

and make it o - kay, I
I'll make you be - lieve that

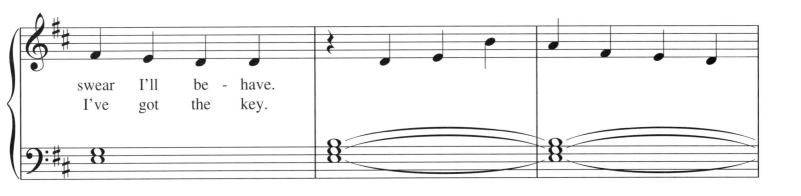

swear I'll be - have.
I've got the key.

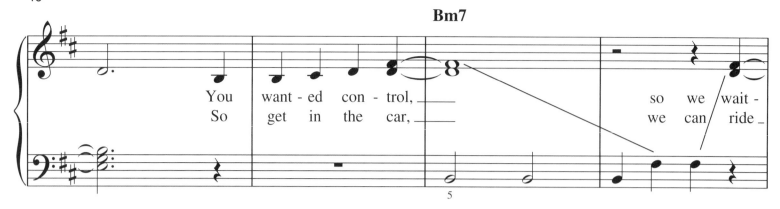

Bm7

You want-ed con-trol, _____ so we wait-
So get in the car, _____ we can ride

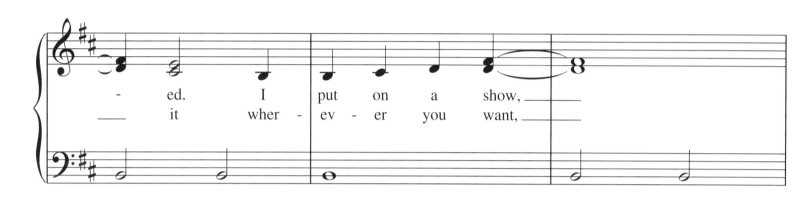

- ed. I put on a show, _____
_____ it wher - ev - er you want, _____

now we're na - ked. You say I'm a kid, _____
get in - side _____ it. And you wan - na steer, _____

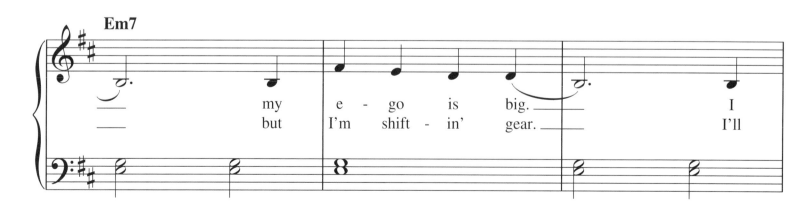

Em7

my e - go is big. _____ I
but I'm shift - in' gear. _____ I'll

don't give a sh**. ____ ____
take it from here. ____ ____
And it goes ____

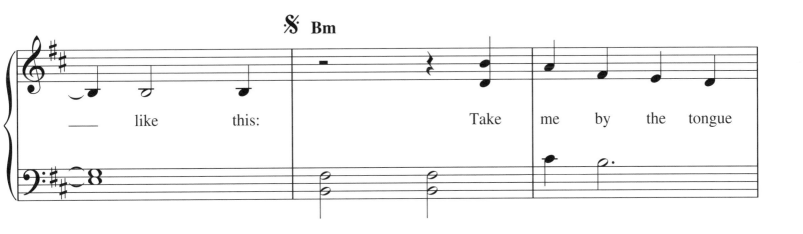

𝄋 **Bm**

____ like this: Take me by the tongue

and I'll know ____ you.   Kiss me 'til you're drunk

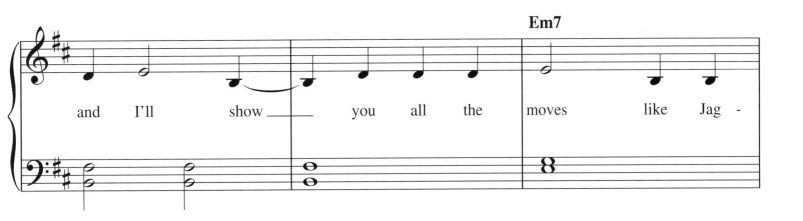

Em7

and I'll show ____ you all the moves like Jag -

ger. I've got the   moves   like Jag -   ger, I've   got the

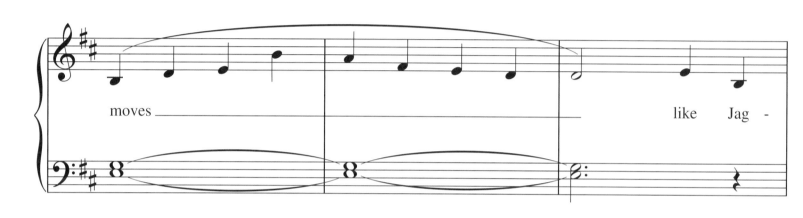

moves _____   like   Jag -

Bm

ger.   I   don't need to try   to con - trol __

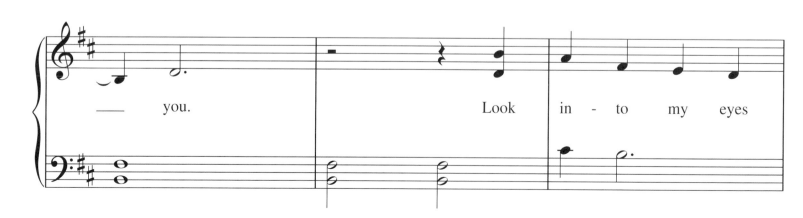

___ you.   Look   in - to   my   eyes

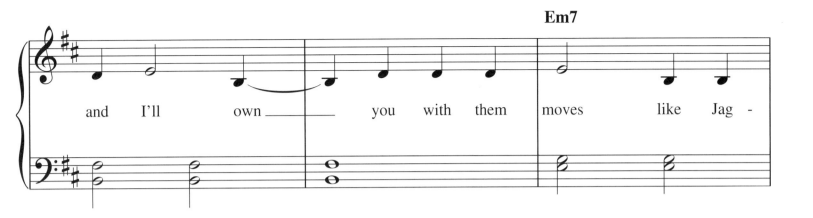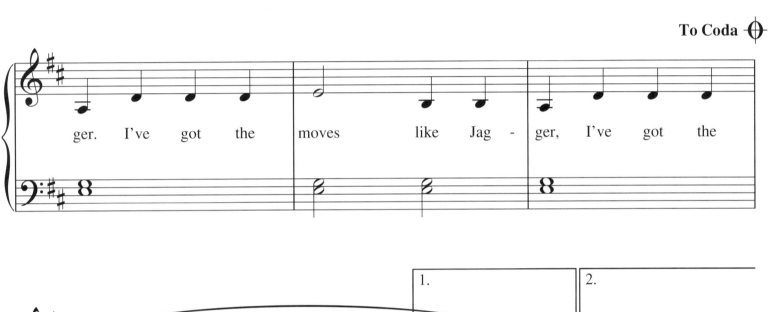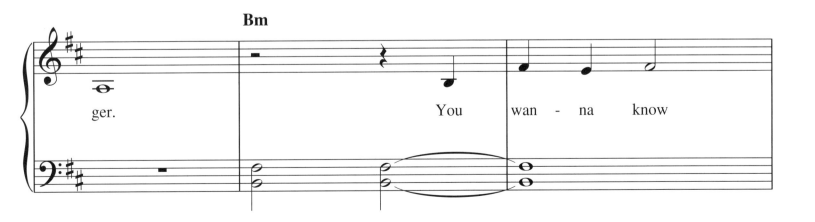

44

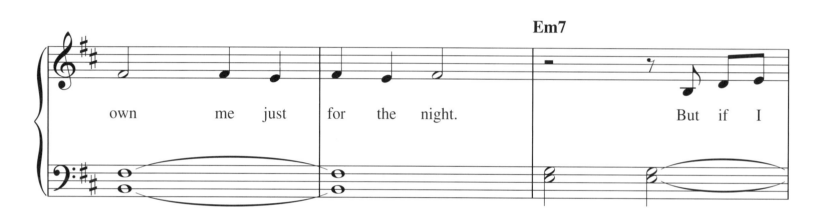

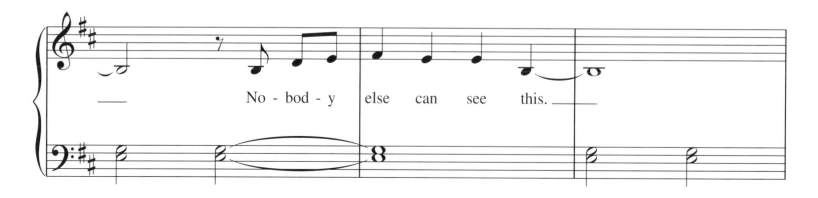

46

else can see this, _____ hey, hey, _____ hey, yeah. _____

D.S. al Coda

CODA

_____ And it goes _____ like this:

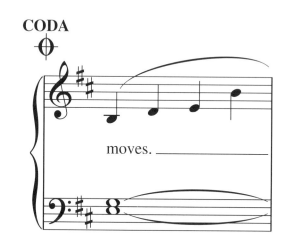

moves. _____

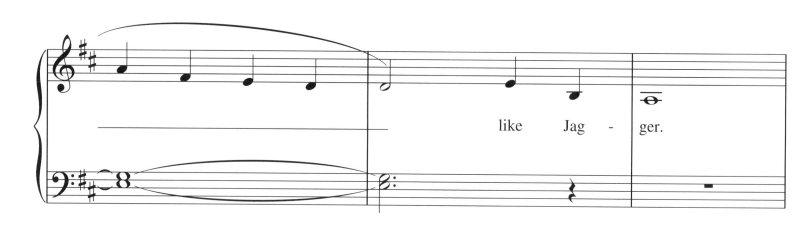

_____ like Jag - ger.

Bm

PARADISE

Words and Music by GUY BERRYMAN,
JON BUCKLAND, WILL CHAMPION,
CHRIS MARTIN and BRIAN ENO

Copyright © 2011 by Universal Music Publishing MGB Ltd. and Opal Ltd.
All Rights for Universal Music Publishing MGB Ltd. in the United States and Canada Administered by Universal Music - MGB Songs
International Copyright Secured   All Rights Reserved

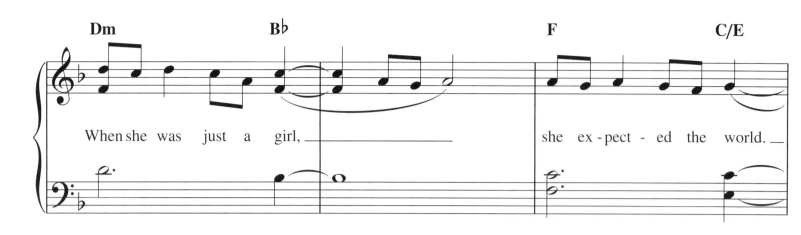

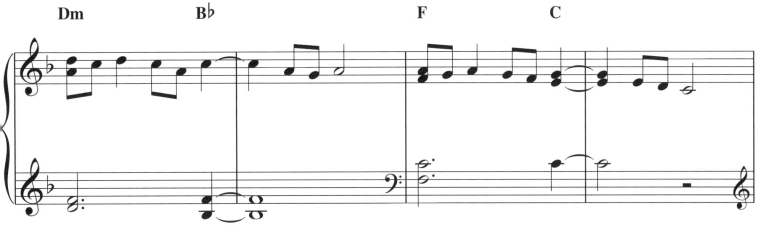

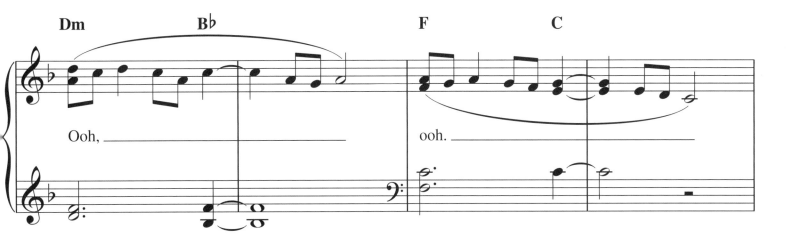

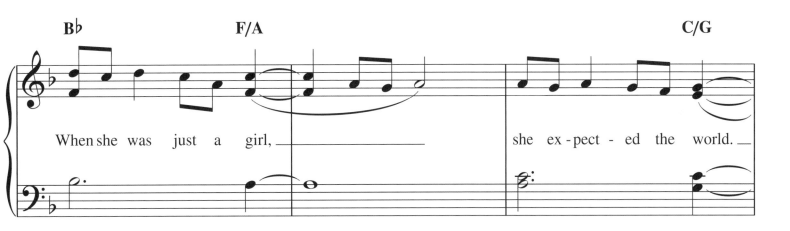

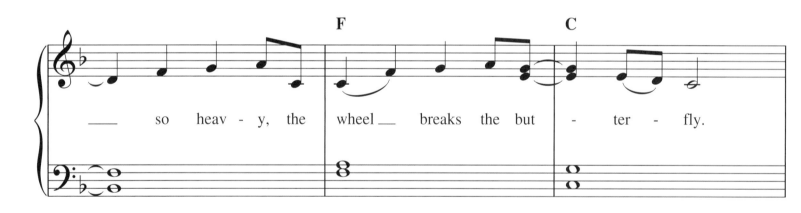

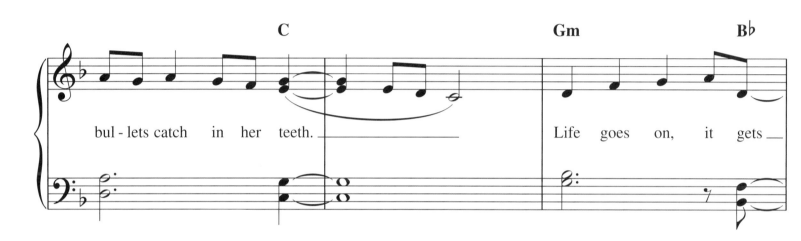

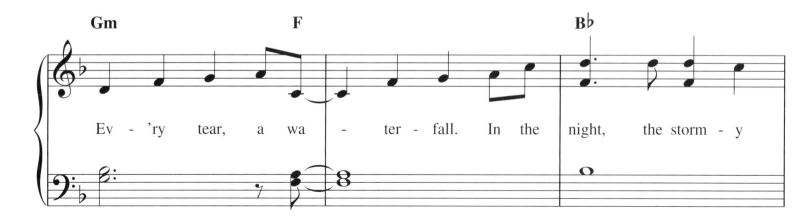

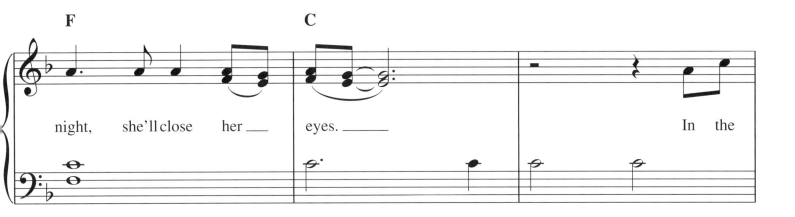

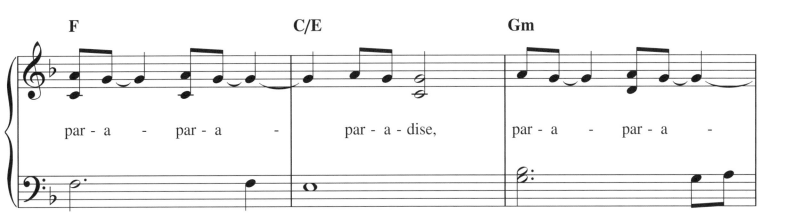

- par - a - dise, oh, _____ oh. She'd dream of

oh, _____ oh.

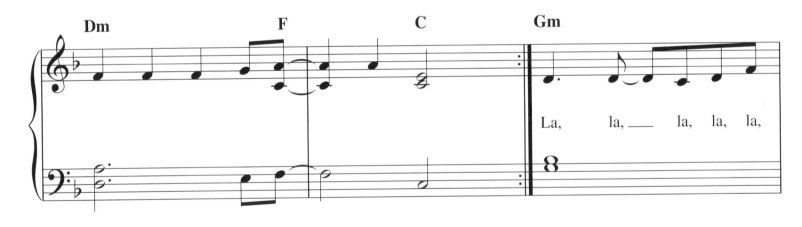

La, la, _____ la, la, la,

la, la, _____ la, la, la, la, la, _____ la, la, la, la, la. And so

53

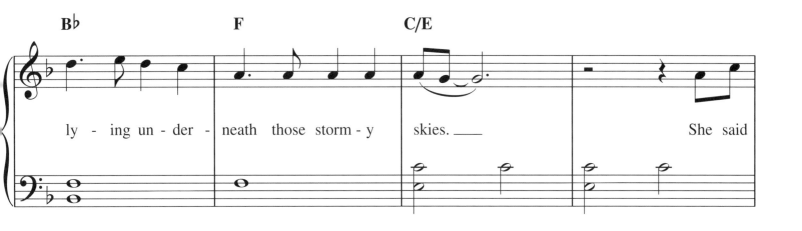

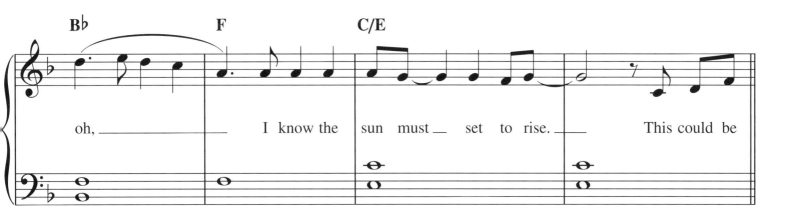

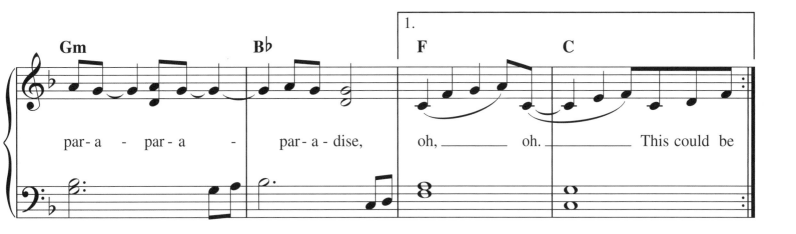

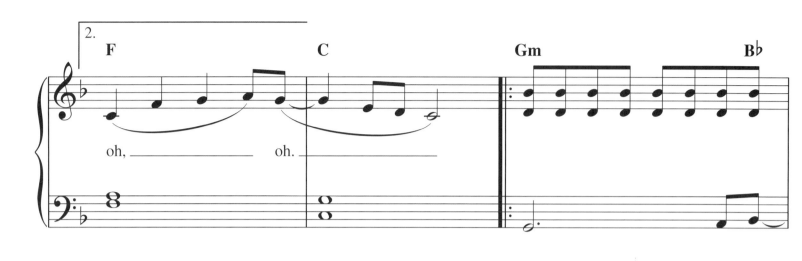

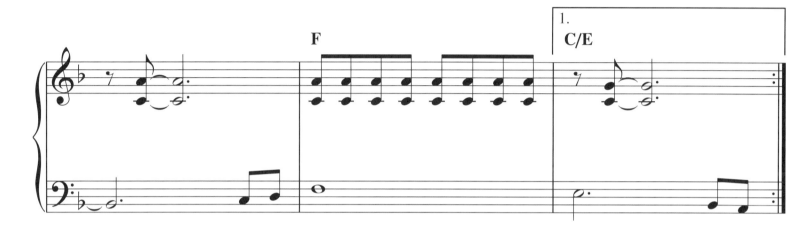

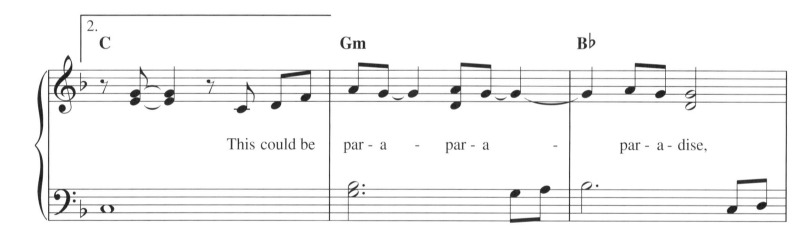

This could be par - a - par - a - par - a - dise,

par - a - par - a - par - a - dise, could be par - a - par - a -

OURS

Words and Music by
TAYLOR SWIFT

Moderately fast

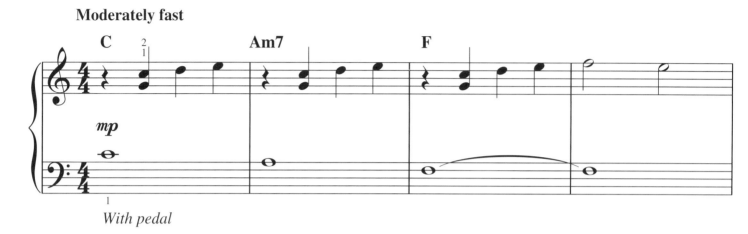

mp

With pedal

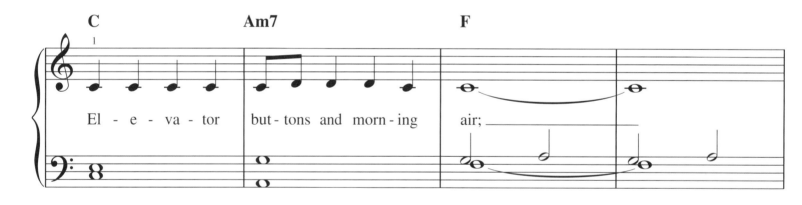

El - e - va - tor but - tons and morn - ing air;

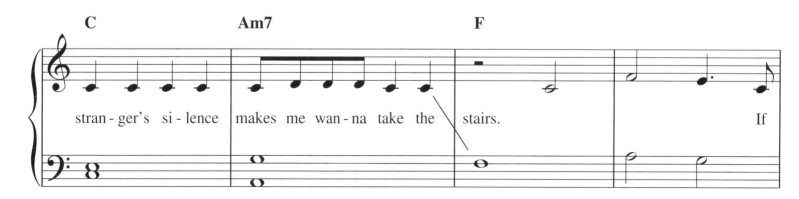

stran - ger's si - lence makes me wan - na take the stairs. If

Copyright © 2011 Sony/ATV Music Publishing LLC and Taylor Swift Music
All Rights Administered by Sony/ATV Music Publishing LLC, 8 Music Square West, Nashville, TN 37203
International Copyright Secured   All Rights Reserved

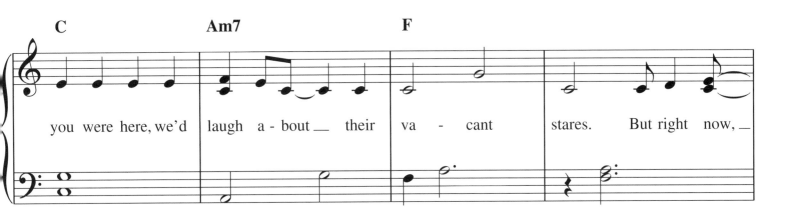

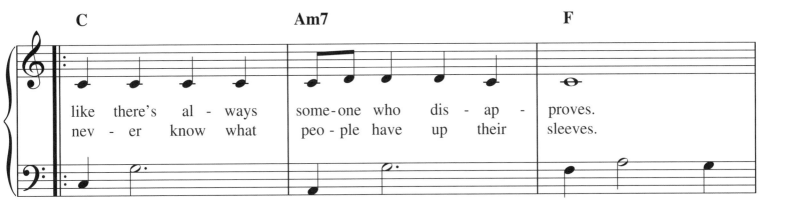

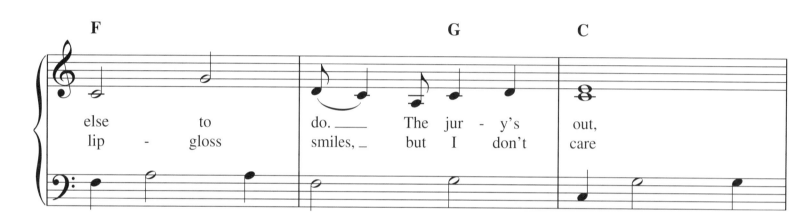

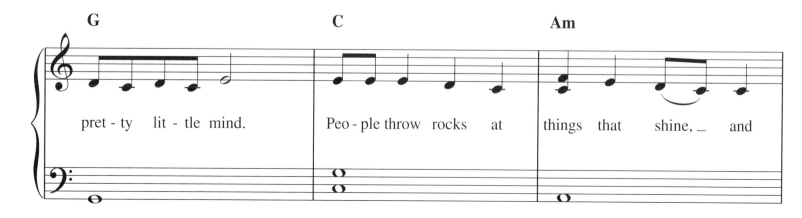

60

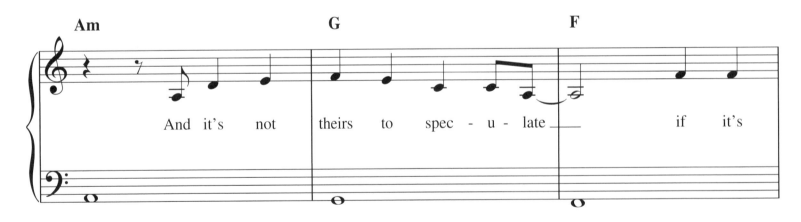

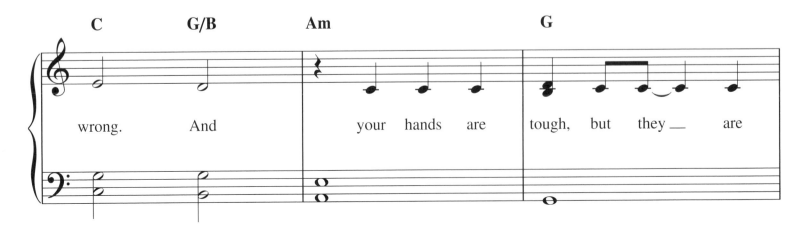

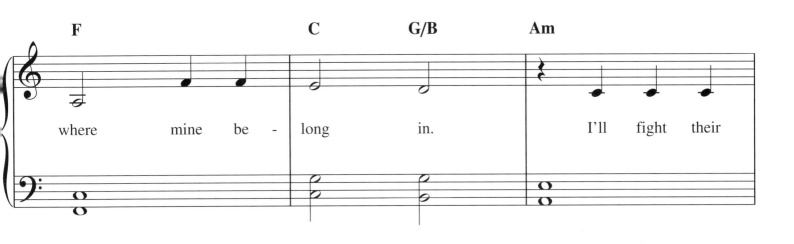

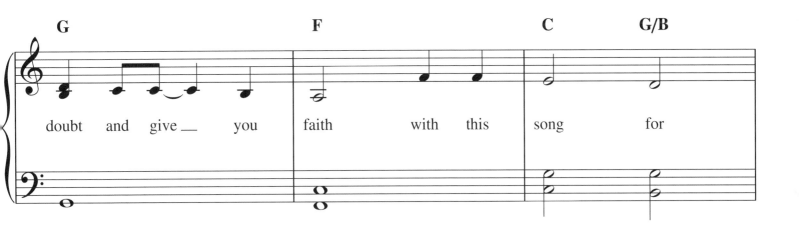

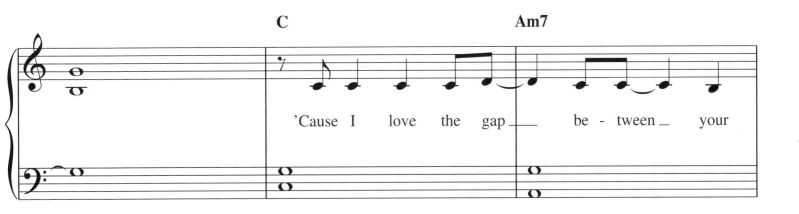

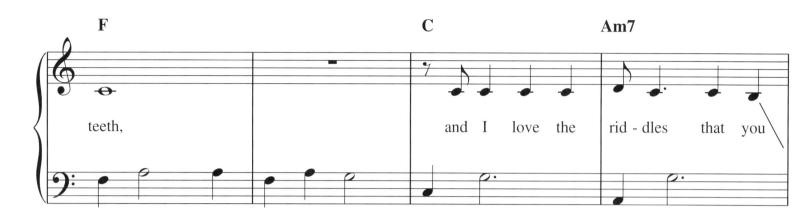

teeth, and I love the rid-dles that you

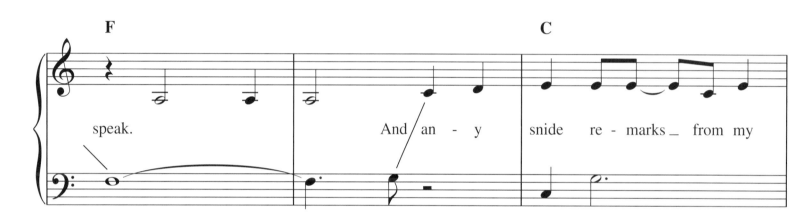

speak. And an - y snide re - marks _ from my

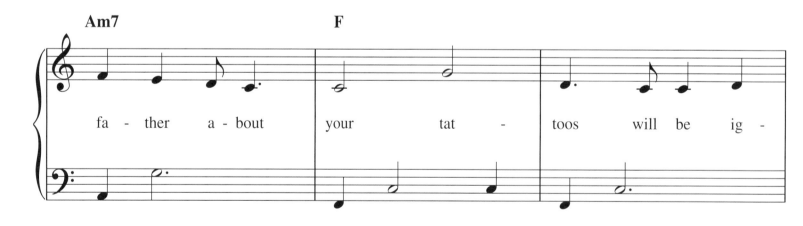

fa - ther a - bout your tat - toos will be ig -

nored 'cause my heart is yours. So

CODA

And don't you wor-ry your pret-ty lit-tle mind.

Peo-ple throw rocks at things that shine, __ but they can't

take what's ours. ___ The stakes are high,

the wa-ter's rough, but this love is ours.

POKER FACE

Words and Music by STEFANI GERMANOTTA
and RedOne

Copyright © 2008 Sony/ATV Music Publishing LLC, House Of Gaga Publishing Inc. and RedOne Productions, LLC
All Rights Administered by Sony/ATV Music Publishing LLC, 8 Music Square West, Nashville, TN 37203
International Copyright Secured   All Rights Reserved

65

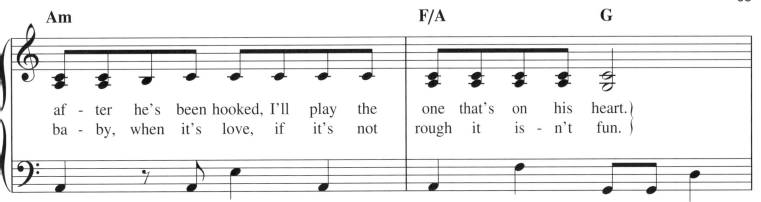

af - ter he's been hooked, I'll play the one that's on his heart.
ba - by, when it's love, if it's not rough it is - n't fun.

Oh, whoa, — oh, oh, oh, ____ oh, oh. I'll get him hot, show

him what I got. ___ Oh, whoa, — oh, oh, oh, ____ oh,

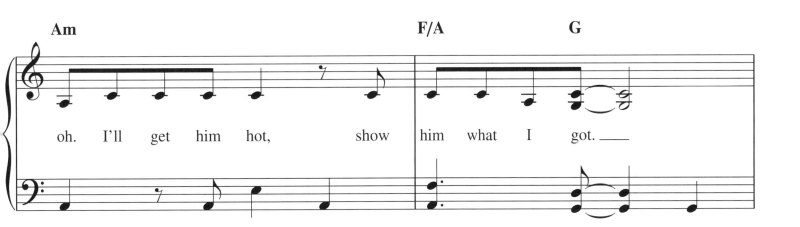

oh. I'll get him hot, show him what I got. ___

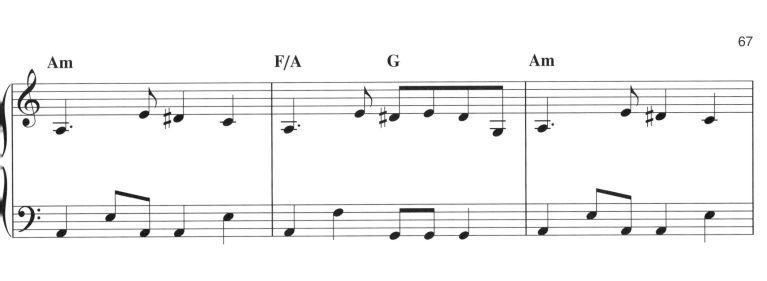

Spoken: I won't tell you | *that I love you, kiss or hug you*

'cause I'm bluf - fin' with my muf - fin. | *I'm not ly - in', I'm just stun - nin'*

with my love glue - gun - nin'. Just | *like a chick in the ca - si - no,*

68

take your bank be - fore I pay you out. I prom - ise this, prom - ise this.

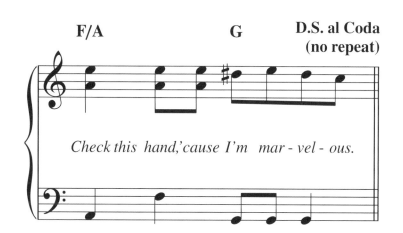

Check this hand,'cause I'm mar - vel - ous.

D.S. al Coda (no repeat)

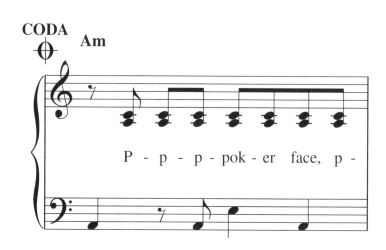

CODA

P - p - p - pok - er face, p -

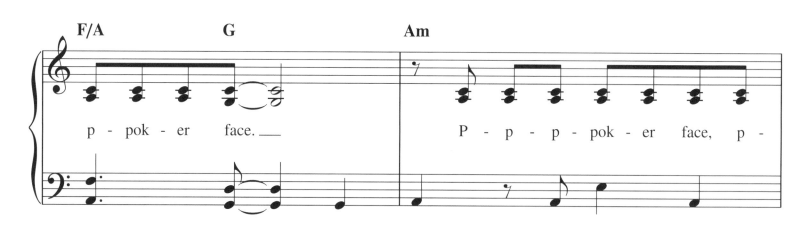

p - pok - er face. ____

P - p - p - pok - er face, p -

p - pok - er face. ____

STRONGER
(What Doesn't Kill You)

Words and Music by GREG KURSTIN,
JORGEN ELOFSSON, DAVID GAMSON
and ALEXANDRA TAMPOSI

Moderate Dance groove

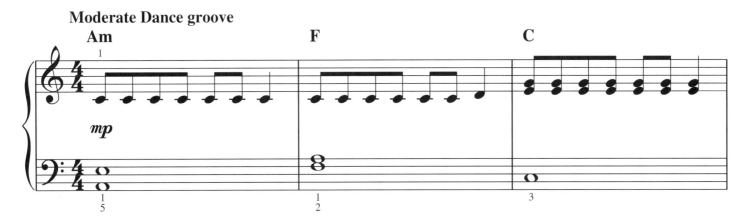

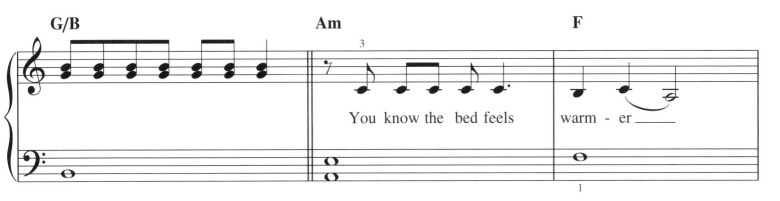

You know the bed feels warm - er

sleep - in' here a - lone. You know I dream in

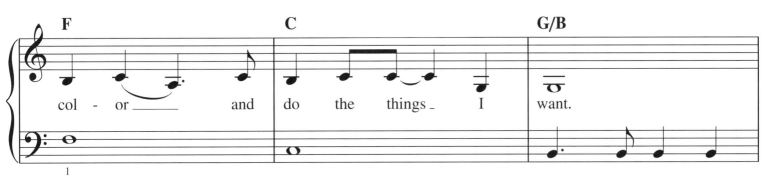

col - or and do the things I want.

© 2011 EMI APRIL MUSIC INC., KURSTIN MUSIC, UNIVERSAL MUSIC PUBLISHING MGB SCANDINAVIA, BMG GOLD SONGS and PERFECT STORM MUSIC GROUP AB
All Rights for KURSTIN MUSIC Controlled and Administered by EMI APRIL MUSIC INC.
All Rights for UNIVERSAL MUSIC PUBLISHING MGB SCANDINAVIA in the United States and Canada Administered by UNIVERSAL MUSIC - CAREERS
All Rights for BMG GOLD SONGS Administered by BMG RIGHTS MANAGEMENT (US) LLC
All Rights for PERFECT STORM MUSIC GROUP AB Administered by SONY/ATV MUSIC PUBLISHING LLC, 8 Music Square West, Nashville, TN 37203
All Rights Reserved   International Copyright Secured   Used by Permission

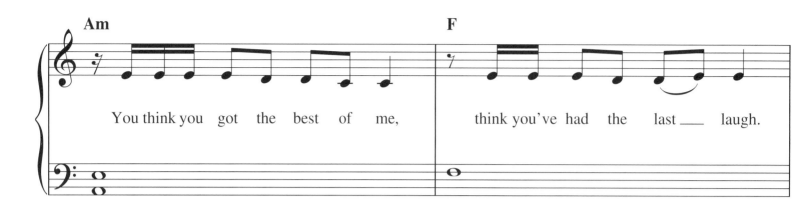

Am ... **F**

You think you got the best of me, think you've had the last ___ laugh.

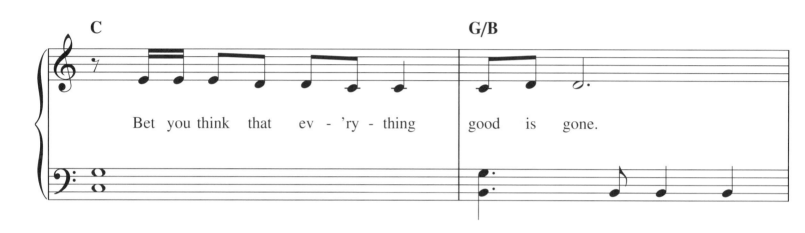

C ... **G/B**

Bet you think that ev - 'ry - thing good is gone.

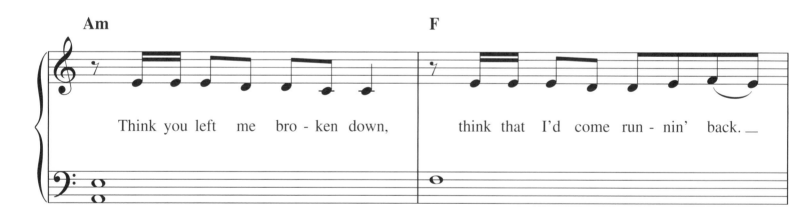

Am ... **F**

Think you left me bro - ken down, think that I'd come run - nin' back. ___

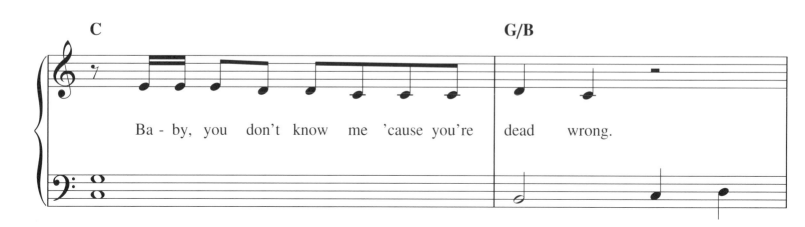

C ... **G/B**

Ba - by, you don't know me 'cause you're dead wrong.

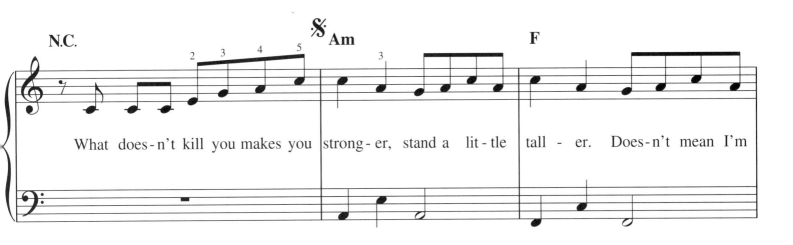

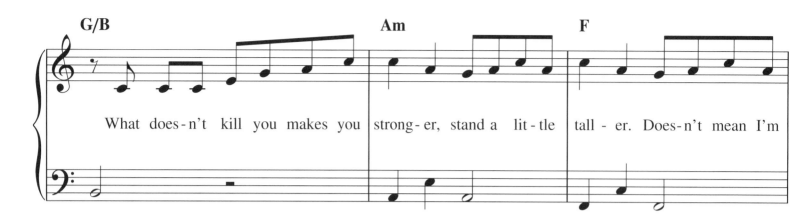

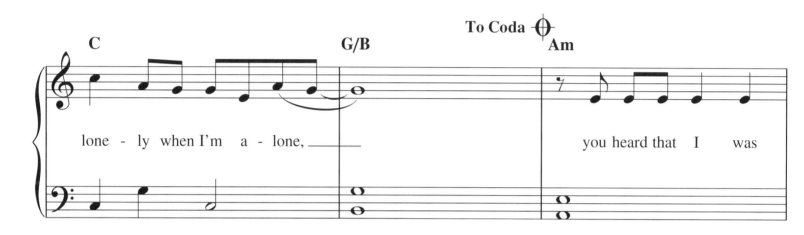

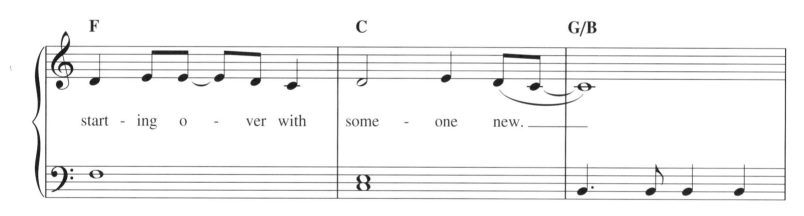

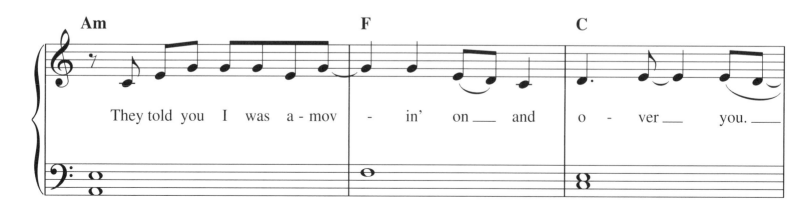

G/B   Am   F

You did-n't think that I'd come back,   I'd come back swing - in'.

C   N.C.   **D.S. al Coda**

You tried to break me. But you   see, what does-n't kill you makes you

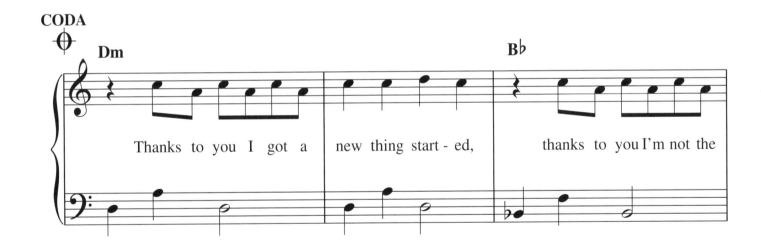

CODA   Dm   B♭

Thanks to you I got a   new thing start - ed,   thanks to you I'm not the

Am

bro - ken - heart - ed. ___   Thanks to you I'm fi - n'ly   think-in' 'bout me.   You

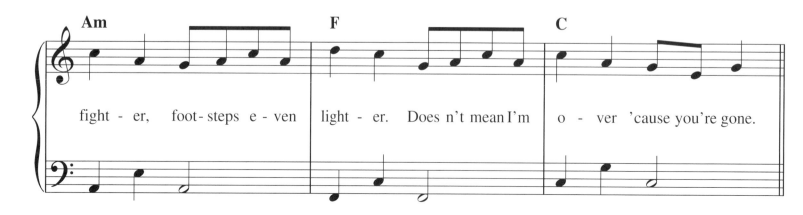

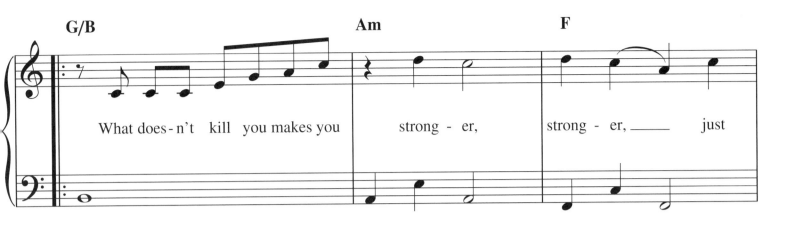

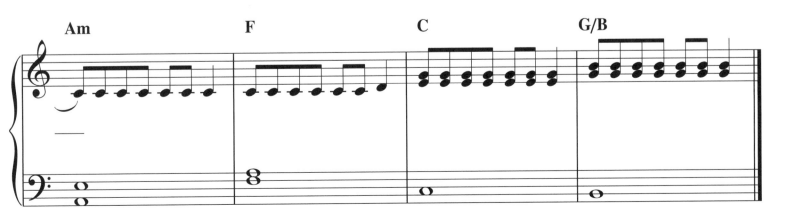

ROLLING IN THE DEEP

Words and Music by ADELE ADKINS
and PAUL EPWORTH

Copyright © 2010, 2011 UNIVERSAL MUSIC PUBLISHING LTD. and EMI MUSIC PUBLISHING LTD.
All Rights for UNIVERSAL MUSIC PUBLISHING LTD. in the U.S. and Canada Controlled and Administered by UNIVERSAL - SONGS OF POLYGRAM INTERNATIONAL, INC.
All Rights for EMI MUSIC PUBLISHING LTD. in the U.S. and Canada Controlled and Administered by EMI BLACKWOOD MUSIC INC.
All Rights Reserved   Used by Permission

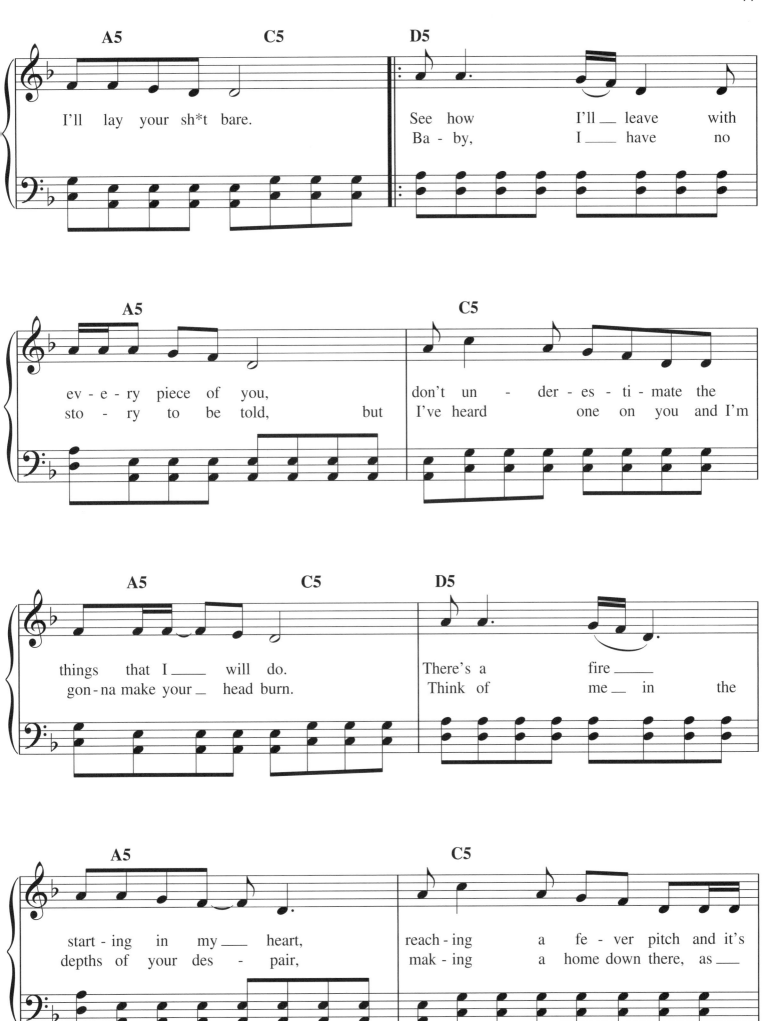

78

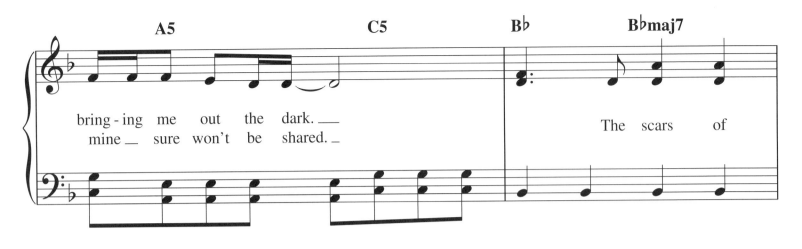

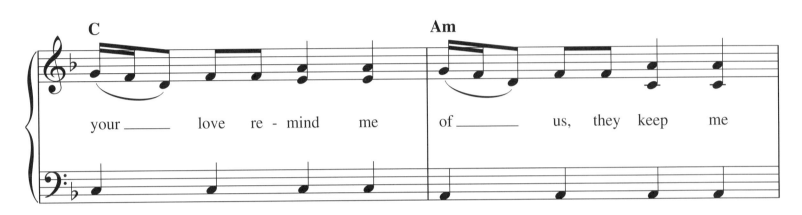

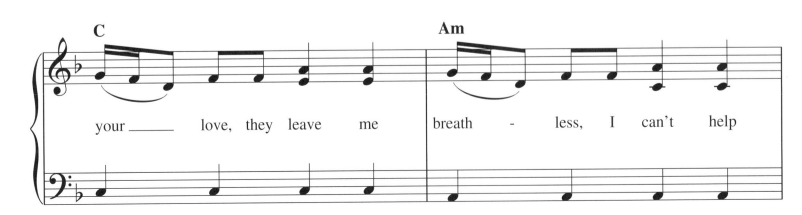

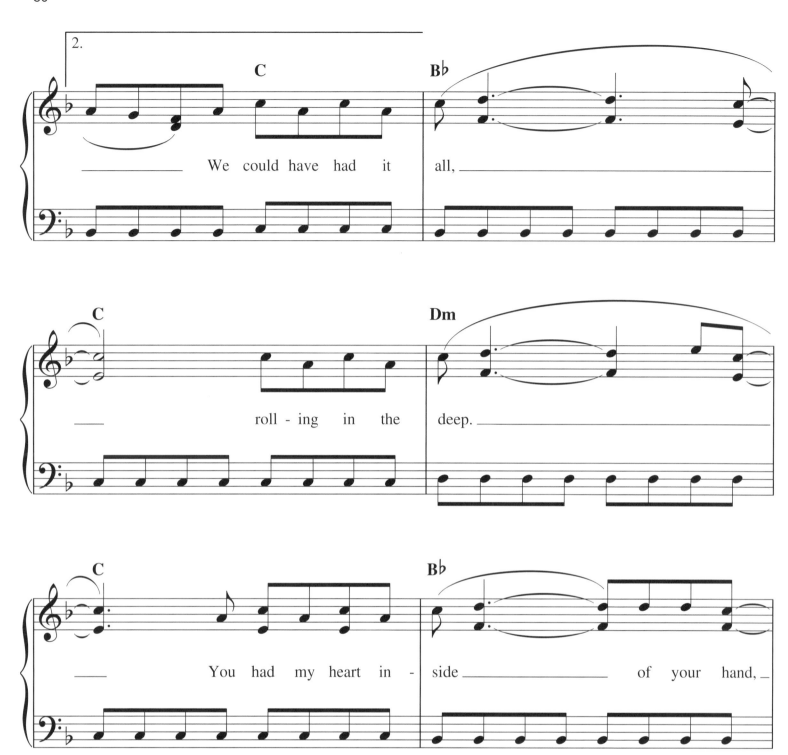

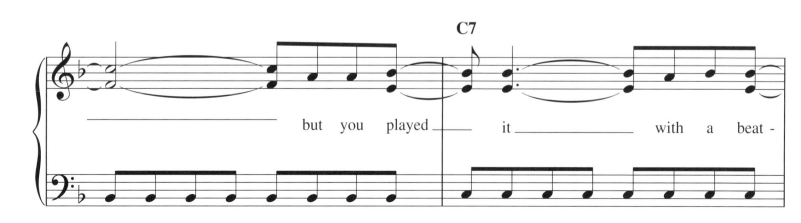

-ing...   Throw your soul _____ through

ev - er - y   o - pen door,   count your bless - ings to

find what you look for.   Turn my sor - row in - to treas-ured gold.   You

pay me back in kind and   reap just what you sow. _____

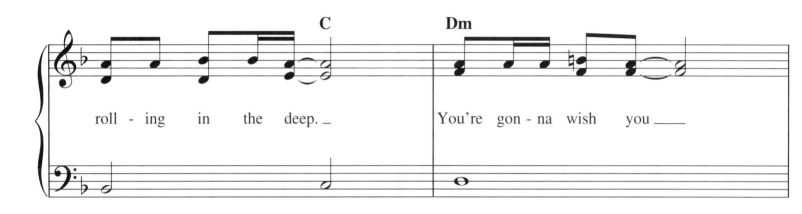

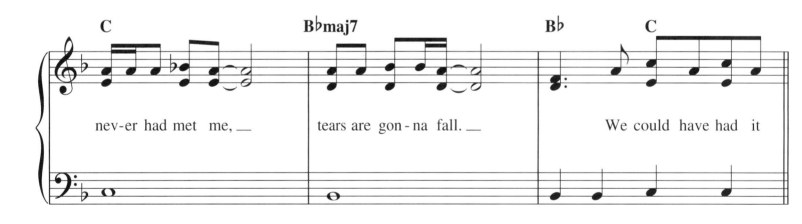

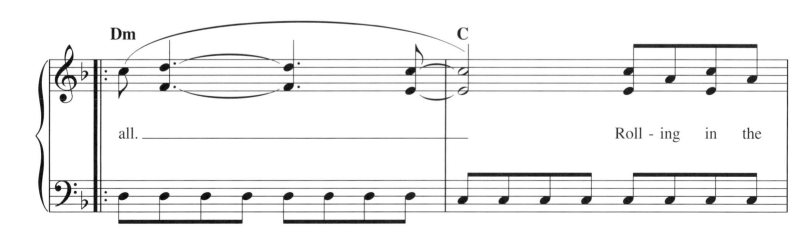

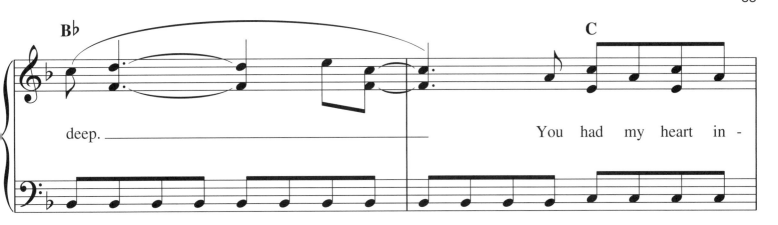

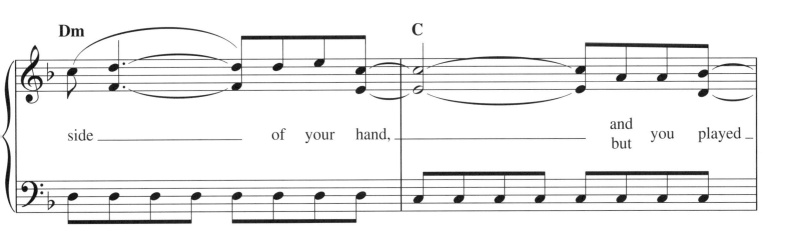

SOMEONE LIKE YOU

Words and Music by ADELE ADKINS
and DAN WILSON

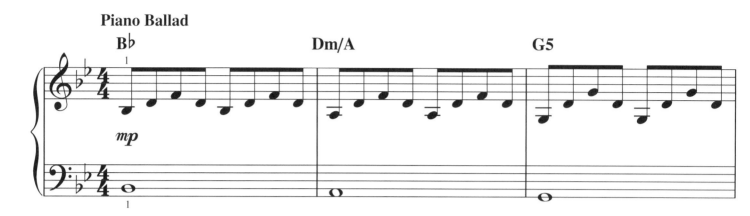

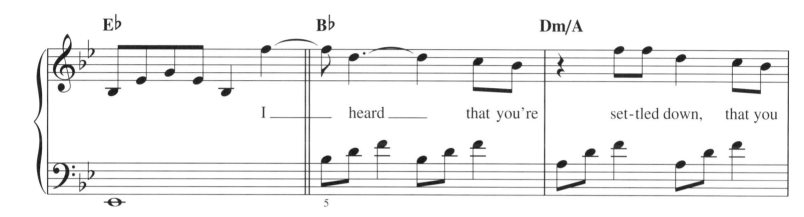

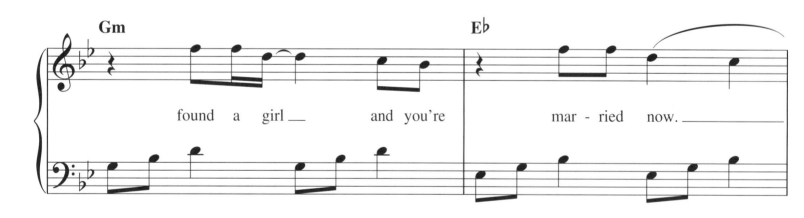

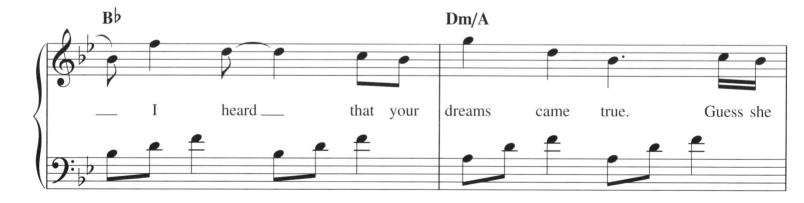

Copyright © 2011 UNIVERSAL MUSIC PUBLISHING LTD., CHRYSALIS MUSIC and SUGAR LAKE MUSIC
All Rights for UNIVERSAL MUSIC PUBLISHING LTD. in the U.S. and Canada Controlled and Administered by UNIVERSAL - SONGS OF POLYGRAM INTERNATIONAL, INC.
All Rights for CHRYSALIS MUSIC and SUGAR LAKE MUSIC Administered by BMG RIGHTS MANAGEMENT (US) LLC
All Rights Reserved   Used by Permission

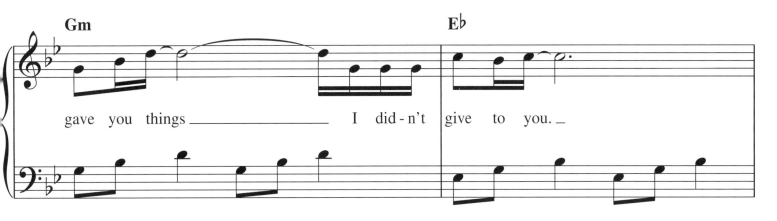

gave you things _____ I did-n't give to you. _

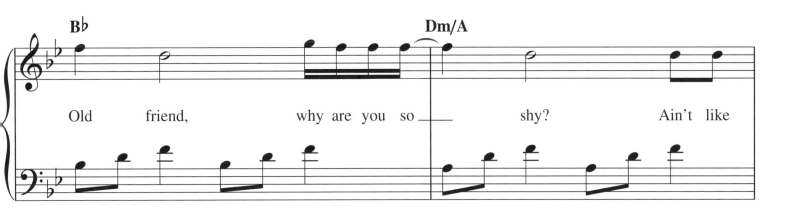

Old friend, why are you so __ shy? Ain't like

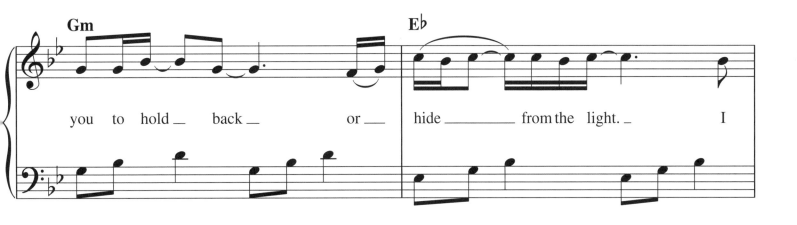

you to hold _ back _ or _ hide _____ from the light. _ I

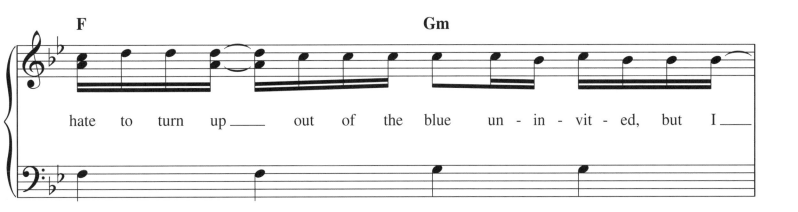

hate to turn up __ out of the blue un-in-vit-ed, but I __

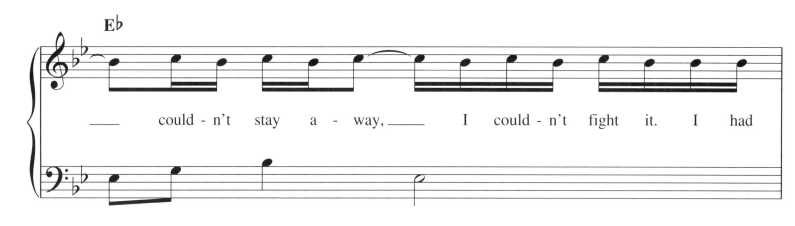

could-n't stay a - way, ____ I could-n't fight it. I had

hoped you'd see my face and that you'd be re - mind - ed that, for

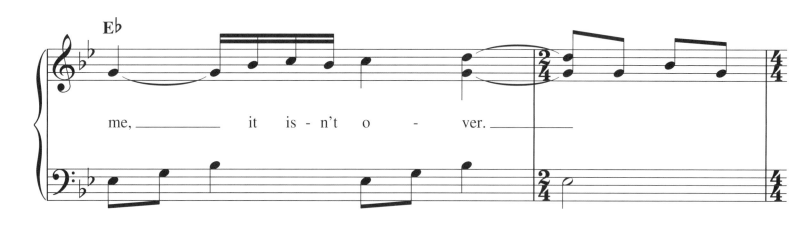

me, _____ it is - n't o - ver. _____

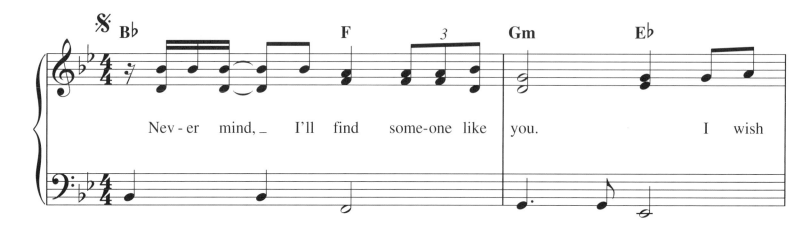

Nev - er mind, _ I'll find some-one like you. I wish

noth - ing but ___ the best for you, too. Don't for -

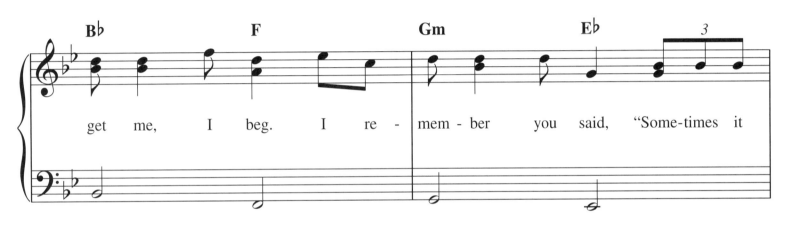

get me, I beg. I re - mem - ber you said, "Some-times it

To Coda ⊕

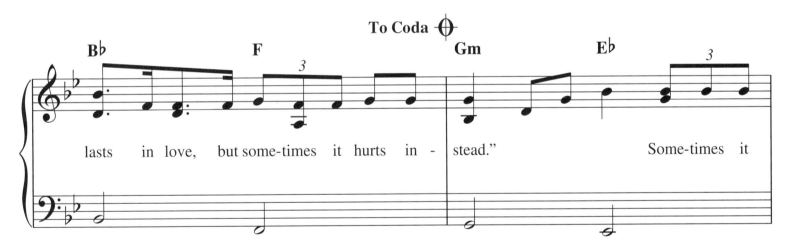

lasts in love, but some-times it hurts in - stead." Some-times it

lasts in love, but some - times it hurts in - stead. _____

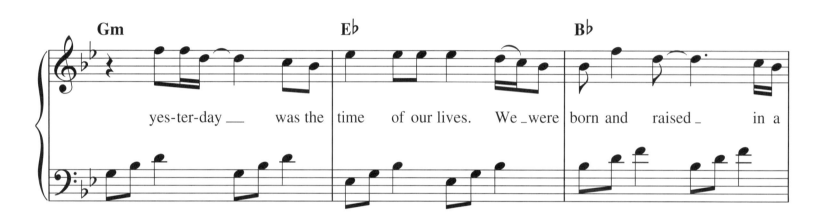

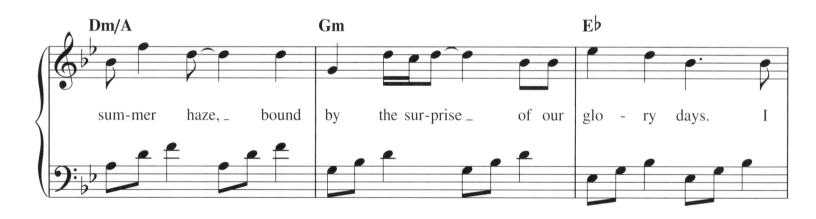

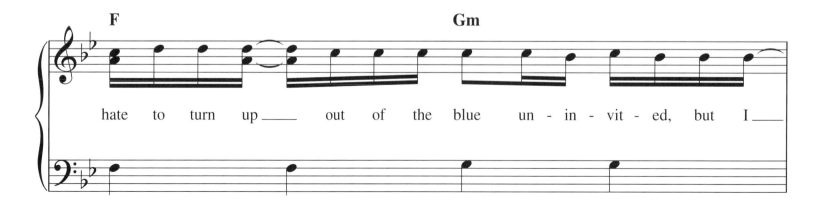

E♭

_____ could-n't stay a - way, _____ I could-n't fight it. I had

F   **Gm**

hoped you'd see my face   and that you'd be re - mind - ed that, for

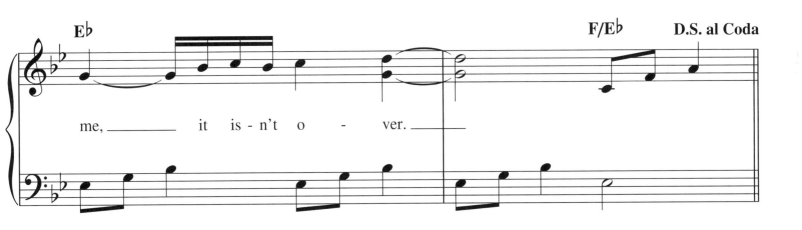

E♭   **F/E♭**   **D.S. al Coda**

me, _____ it is - n't o - ver. _____

CODA   **Gm**   **E♭maj7**   **F/C**

stead." _____

Noth-ing com-pares, no wor-ries or cares, re -

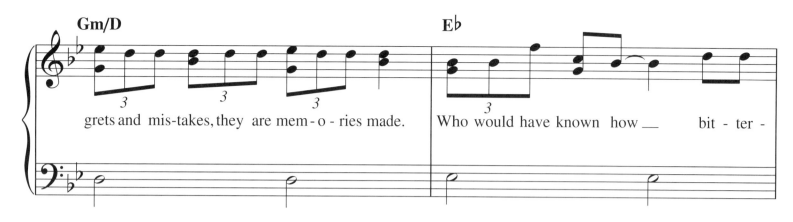

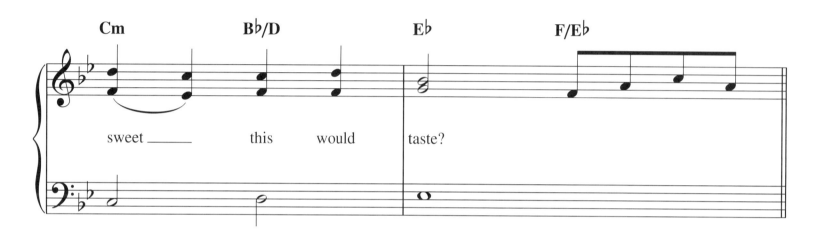

mem - ber   you said, "Some-times it   lasts   in love,   but some-times   it hurts   in -

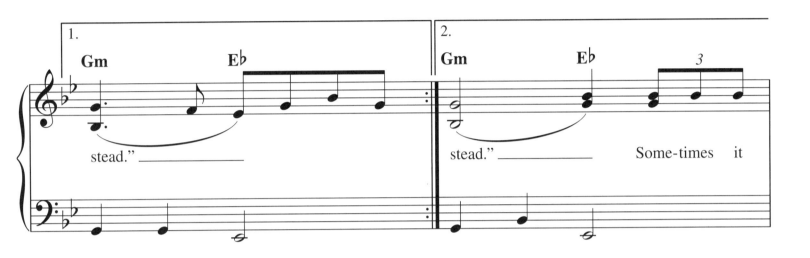

1.

stead." _____   2.

stead." _____   Some-times   it

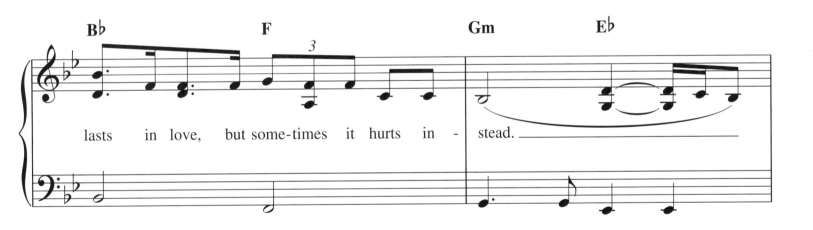

lasts   in love,   but some-times   it hurts   in -   stead. _____

A THOUSAND YEARS

from the Summit Entertainment film THE TWILIGHT SAGA: BREAKING DAWN - Part 1

Words and Music by DAVID HODGES
and CHRISTINA PERRI

Moderately, in one

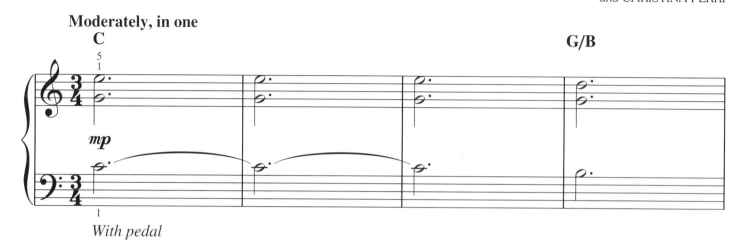

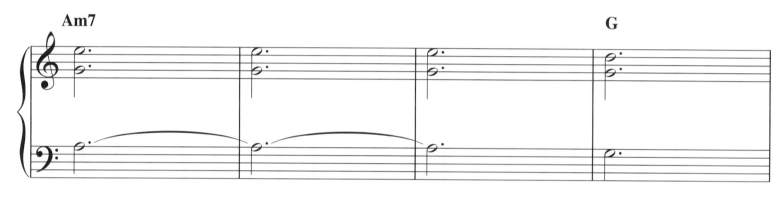

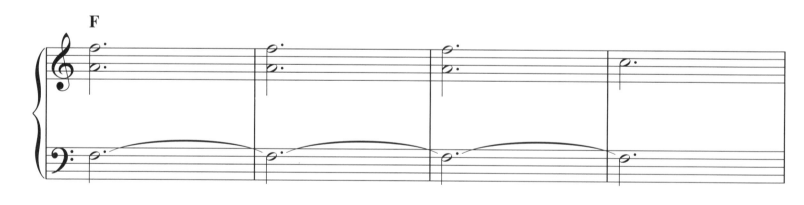

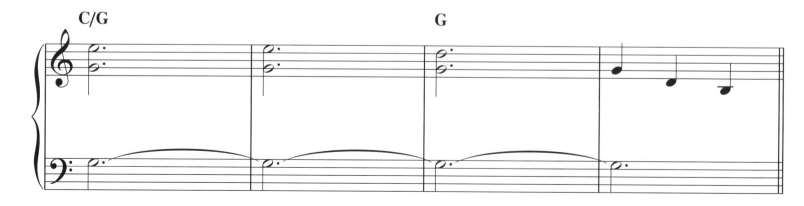

© 2011 EMI BLACKWOOD MUSIC INC., 12:06 PUBLISHING, MISS PERRI LANE PUBLISHING and SUMMIT BASE CAMP FILM MUSIC
All Rights for 12:06 PUBLISHING Controlled and Administered by EMI BLACKWOOD MUSIC INC.
All Rights Reserved   International Copyright Secured   Used by Permission

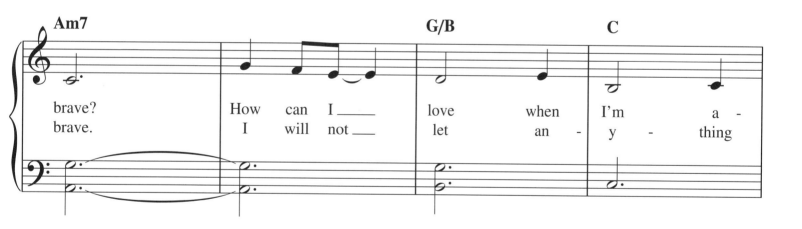

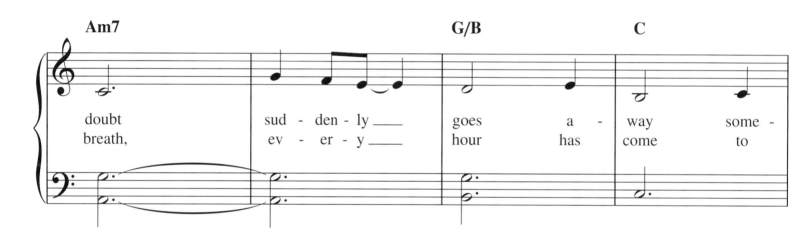

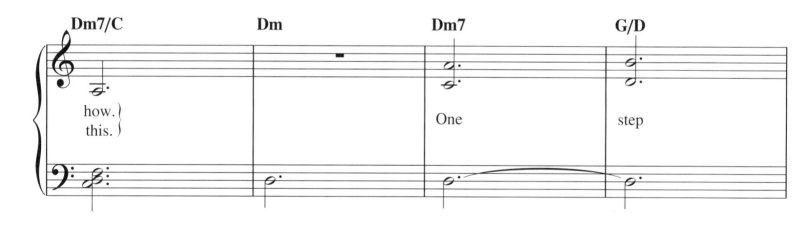

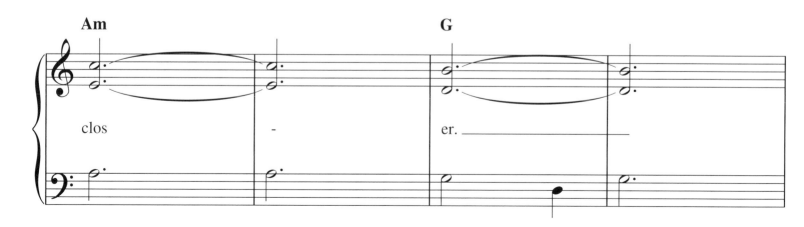

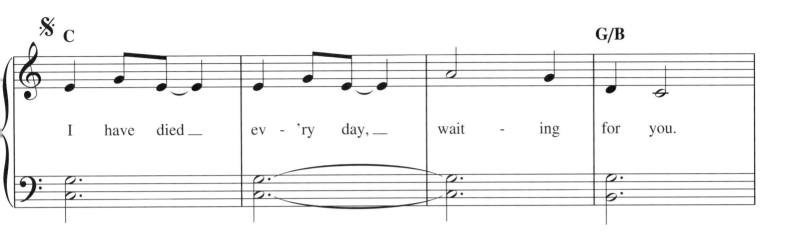

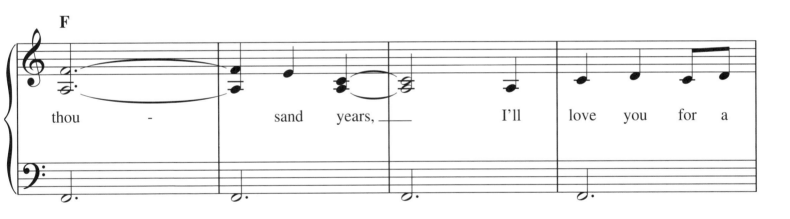

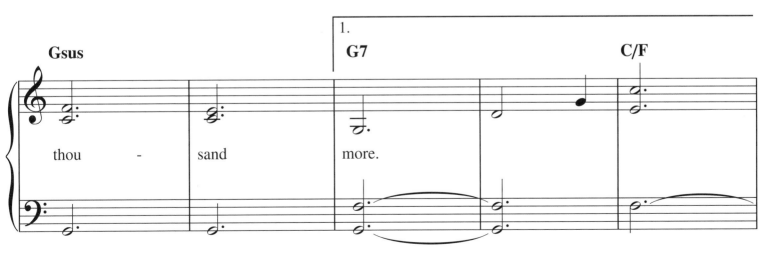

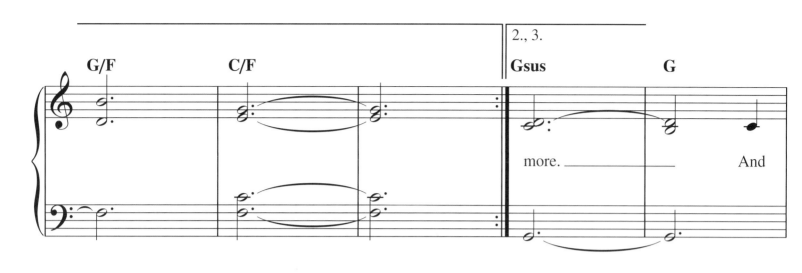

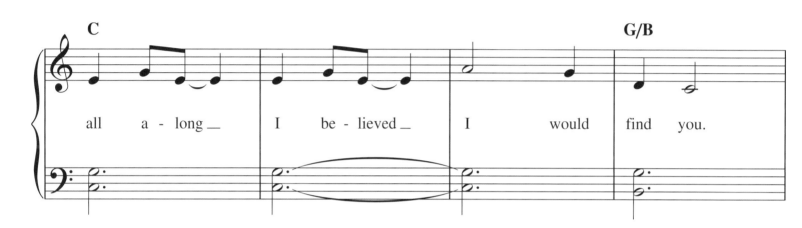

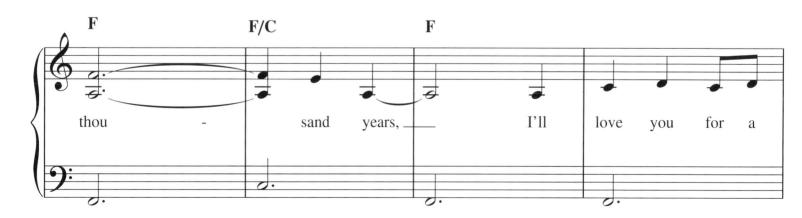

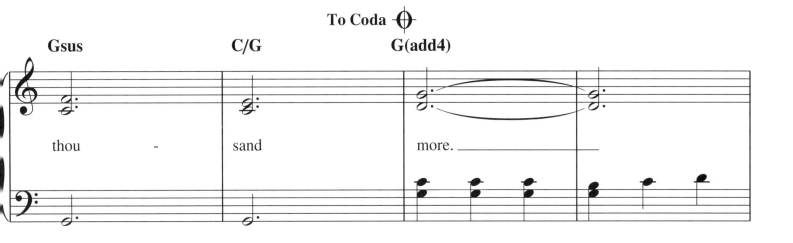

To Coda

Gsus C/G G(add4)

thou - sand more.

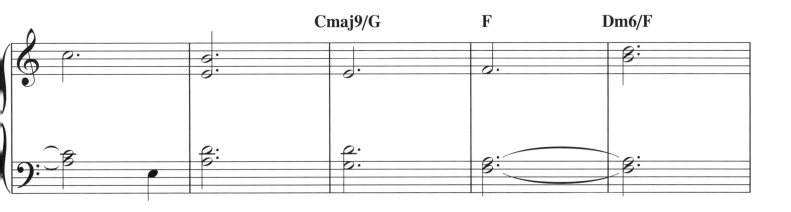

C Cmaj7/D C/G Am

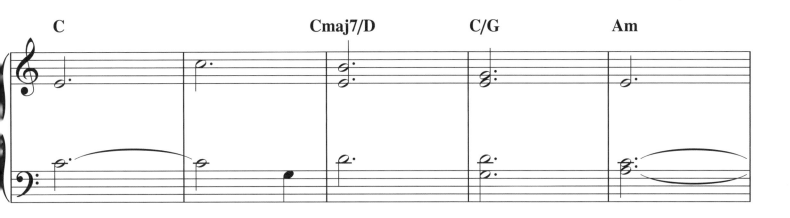

Cmaj9/G F Dm6/F

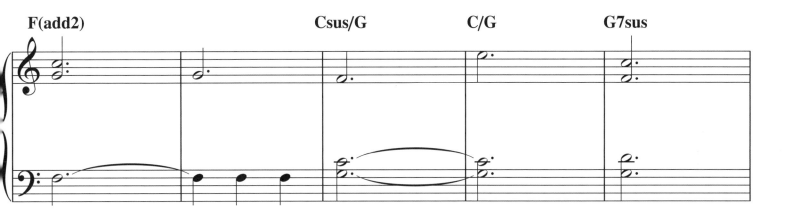

F(add2) Csus/G C/G G7sus

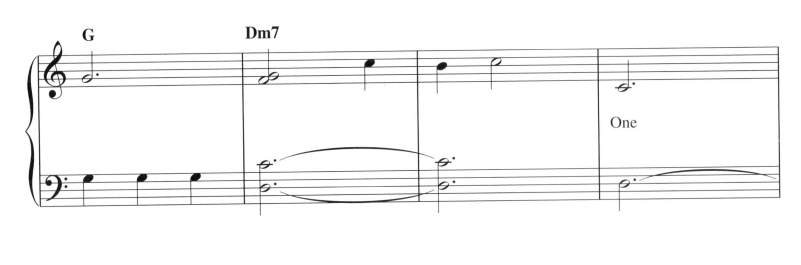

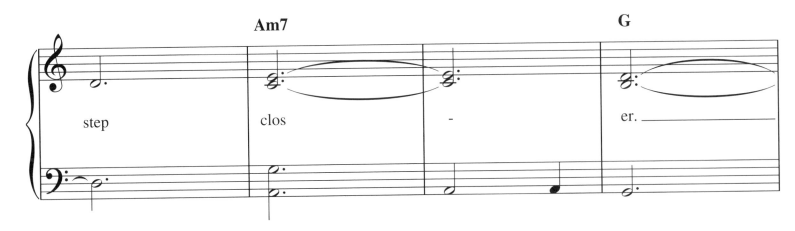

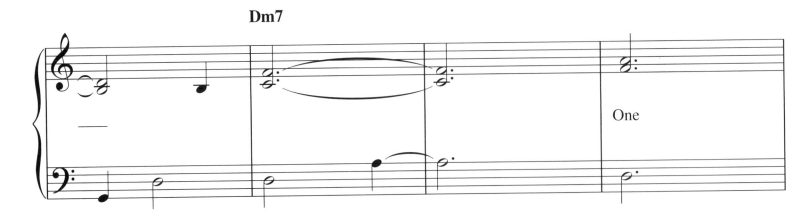

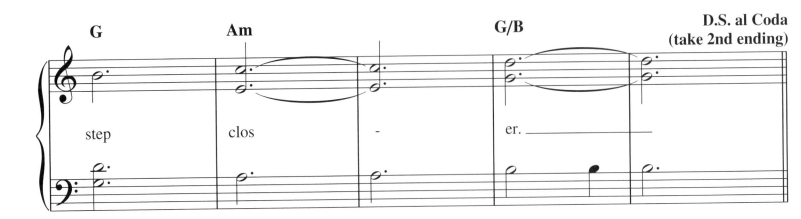

WE ARE YOUNG

Words and Music by JEFF BHASKER,
NATHANIEL RUESS, ANDREW DOST
and JACK ANTONOFF

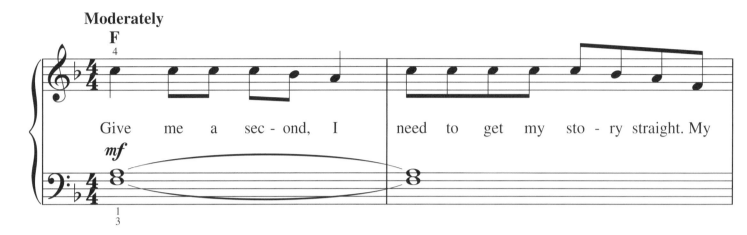

Give me a sec-ond, I need to get my sto-ry straight. My

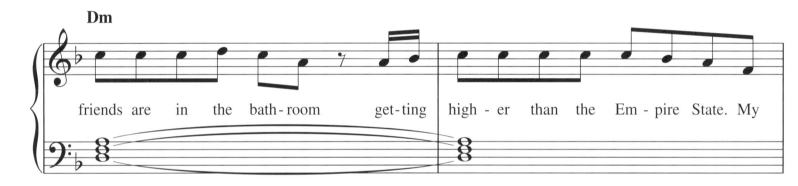

friends are in the bath-room get-ting high-er than the Em-pire State. My

lov-er, she's wait-ing for me just a-cross the bar. My seat's been

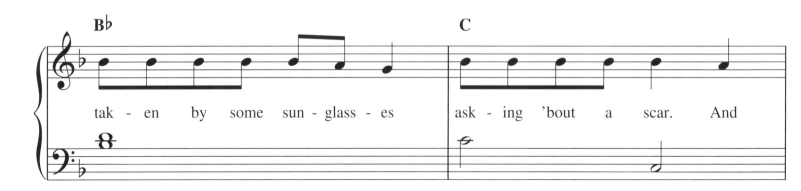

tak-en by some sun-glass-es ask-ing 'bout a scar. And

Copyright © 2011 Sony/ATV Music Publishing LLC, Way Above Music, WB Music Corp., Bearvon Music, FBR Music, Rough Art and Shira Lee Lawrence Rick Music
All Rights on behalf of Sony/ATV Music Publishing LLC and Way Above Music Administered by Sony/ATV Music Publishing LLC
All Rights on behalf of Bearvon Music and FBR Music Administered by WB Music Corp.
International Copyright Secured   All Rights Reserved

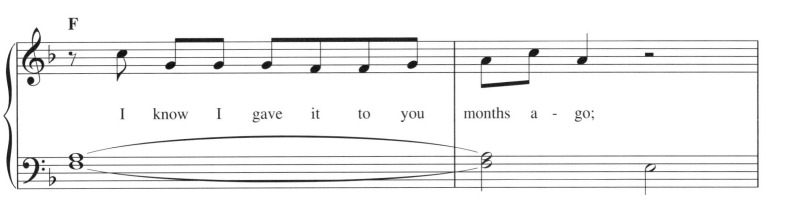

I know I gave it to you months a - go;

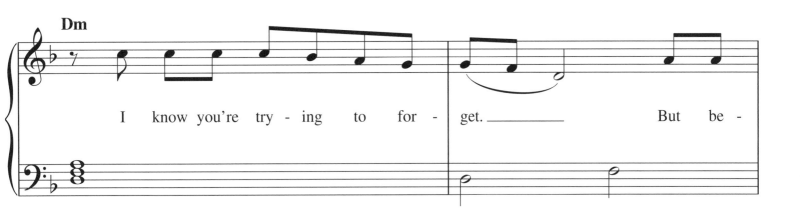

I know you're try - ing to for - get. _____ But be -

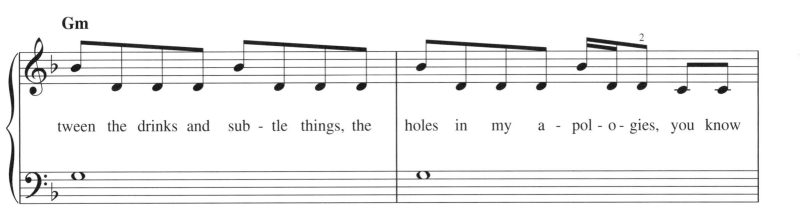

tween the drinks and sub - tle things, the holes in my a - pol - o - gies, you know

I'm try - ing hard to take it back. So, if by the time the bar clos - es and you

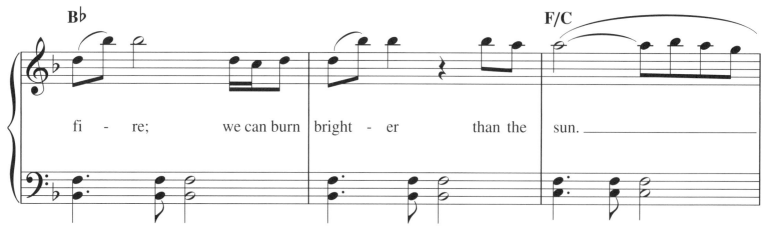

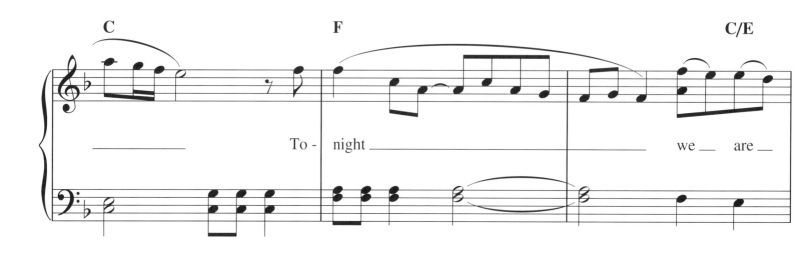

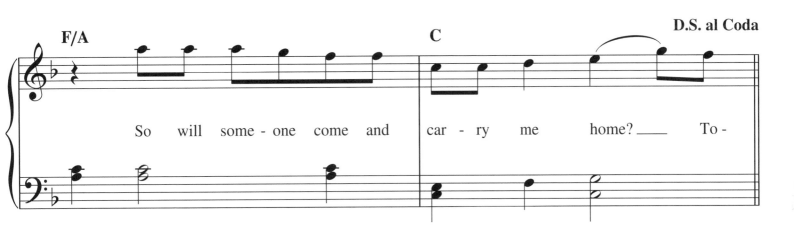

WHAT MAKES YOU BEAUTIFUL

Words and Music by SAVAN KOTECHA,
RAMI YACOUB and CARL FALK

Moderate Pop

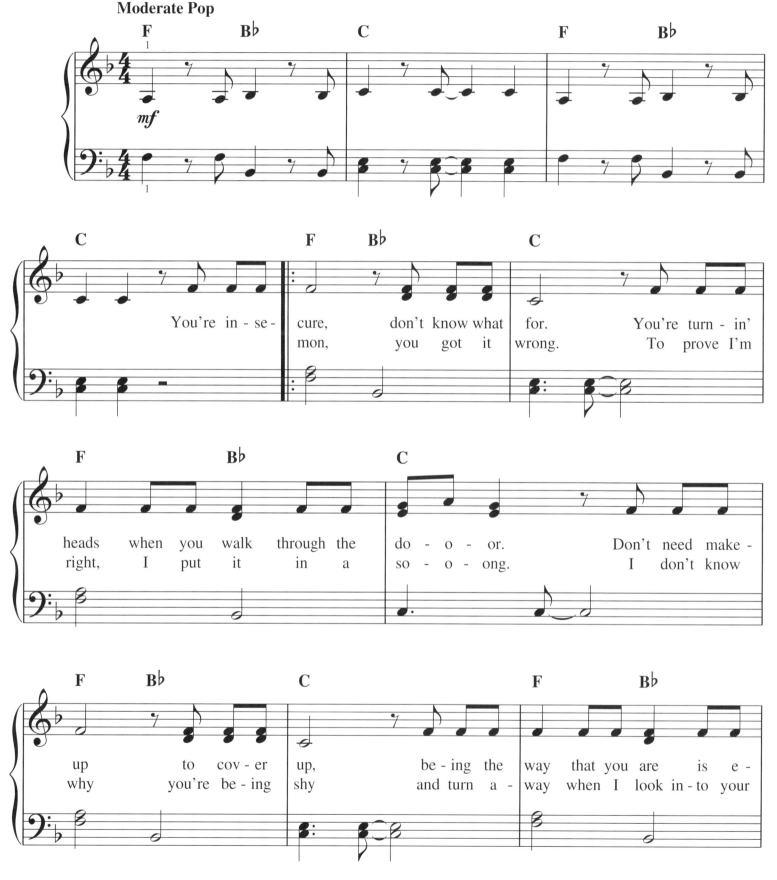

© 2011 EMI APRIL MUSIC INC., MR KANANI SONGS, RAMI PRODUCTIONS AB and AIR CHRYSALIS SCANDINAVIA AB
All Rights for MR KANANI SONGS Controlled and Administered by EMI APRIL MUSIC INC.
All Rights for RAMI PRODUCTIONS AB Administered by KOBALT MUSIC PUBLISHING AMERICA, INC.
All Rights for AIR CHRYSALIS SCANDINAVIA AB Administered by BMG RIGHTS MANAGEMENT (US) LLC
All Rights Reserved   International Copyright Secured   Used by Permission

108

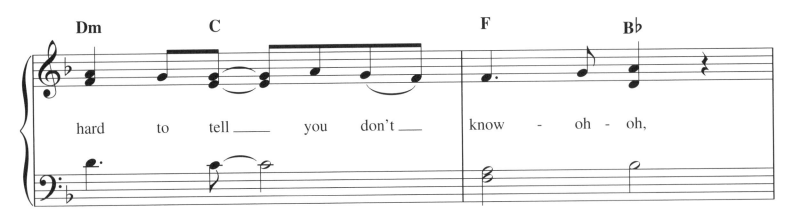

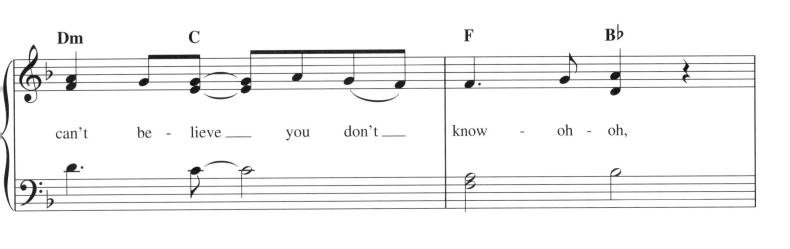

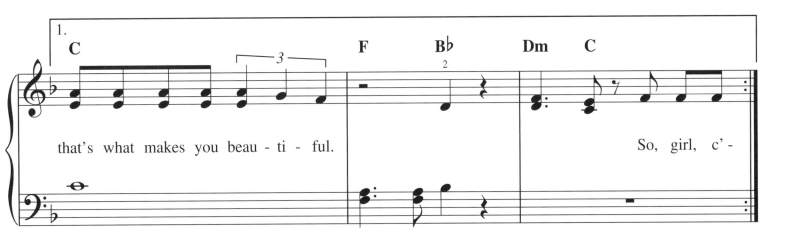

na, na, ___ na. Na, na, na, na, na, na.

Na, na, na, na, na, na, na, na, ___ na. Na, na, na, na, na, na.

Ba - by, you light up my world like no - bod - y else. _ The way that

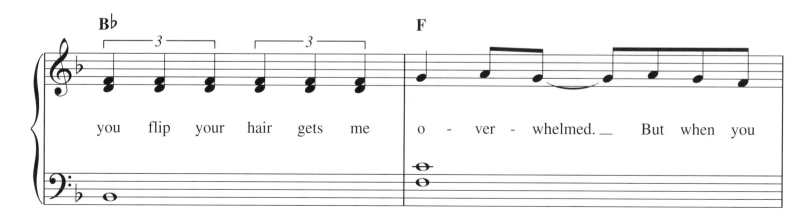

you flip your hair gets me o - ver - whelmed. _ But when you

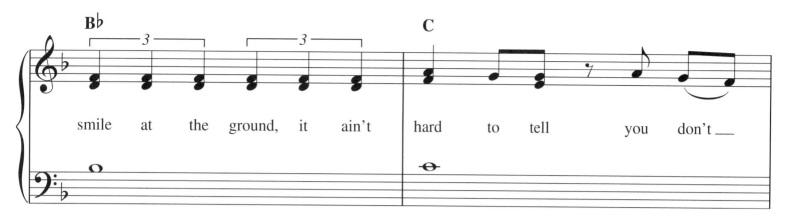

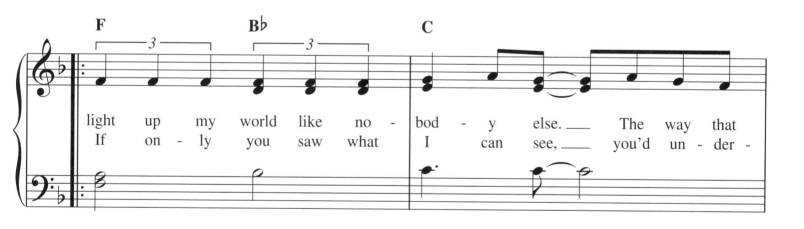

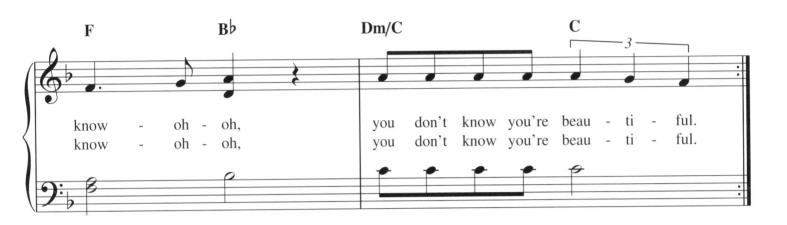

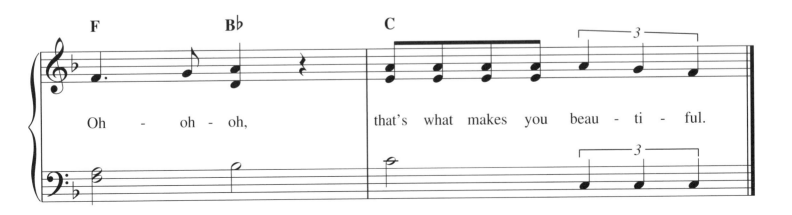